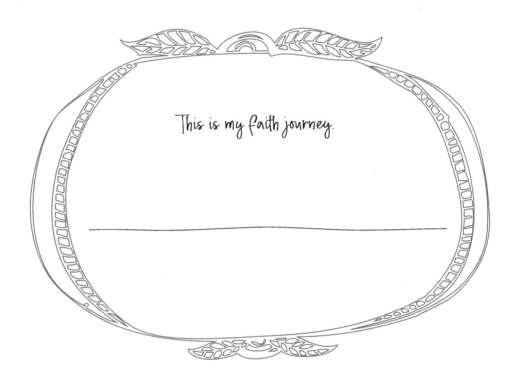

This is my faith journey.

Exploring the Catholic Classics: How Spiritual Reading Can Help You Grow in Wisdom

Nihil obstat:
　　Rev. Timothy Hall,
　　Censor librorum
　　September 15, 2018

Imprimatur:
　　†Most Rev. John M. Quinn,
　　Bishop of Winona
　　September 15, 2018

24 23 22 21 20 19　　2 3 4 5 6 7 8 9

Cover, interior design and composition by Laurie Nelson, Agápe Design Studios.
Graphic elements: © iStockphoto.com, © Adobe Stock

Copy editing by Karen Carter.

ISBN: 978-1-68192-500-4 (Inventory No. T2389)
LCCN: 2019939976

Stay Connected Journals for Catholic Women are published by Our Sunday Visitor Publishing Division, 200 Noll Plaza, Huntington, IN 46750; 1-800-348-2440; www.osv.com.

Acknowledgments

Scripture texts in this work are taken from the New American Bible, revised edition © 2010, 1991, 1986, 1970 Confraternity of Christian Doctrine, Washington, D.C. and are used by permission of the copyright owner. All Rights Reserved. No part of the New American Bible may be reproduced in any form without permission in writing from the copyright owner.

Quotes from the *Catechism of the Catholic Church* are taken from the English translation of the Catechism of the Catholic Church for the United States of America, 2nd ed. Copyright 1997 by United States Catholic Conference— Libreria Editrice Vaticana

Journals for Catholic Women

Exploring the Catholic Classics:

How Spiritual Reading Can Help You Grow in Wisdom

Tiffany Walsh

Acknowledgments

Writing this Scripture study was a labor of love, and I could not have completed it without the support of some important people in my life. I am so grateful to Allison for choosing me to participate in this project and for believing in me! Deanna, also, provided invaluable editing feedback, and I absolutely loved working with her!

My colleagues and friends at my library always root for me in my writing endeavors, and they make me laugh every single day. Laughter is such a key ingredient to all successful creative ventures! Frankly, it is an essential part of a happy life. For this, I thank Cindy, Keith, Bryan, Molly, and Nicole. My boss, Cindi, has provided unfailing support to all of my writing ideas and projects, and I know that God placed her in my life for a reason!

God has, indeed, blessed me with many beautiful friendships. Sam, Allison, Nancy, Stacy, Brandy, and Tracy, I cannot imagine my life without you ladies in it. You each provide me with daily joy and happiness. Also, my Oasis dance girls, who have given me inspiration beyond measure. My family, as well, loves me without conditions and are emotionally beside me every day of my journey in this life—these are my mom and dad, Judy and David, and my sweet sisters, Rhonda and Shauna'h.

Finally, I can do nothing without the love and support of my husband, Mike. We have loved each other for nearly sixteen years, and it feels like that span of time has passed in the mere blink of an eye. He is my daily source of creative inspiration, my confidante, and the love of my life. We are raising our two beautiful children, Henry and Anne, together, and it is an adventure of epic proportions! I am so grateful that I get to share this experience with him. God has blessed me so abundantly in my marriage.

Table of Contents

Introduction to the Catholic Classics. 1

1: The Imitation of Christ 7

2: The Story of a Soul 27

3: The Way of Perfection. 47

4: Introduction to the Devout Life. 69

5: Essays on Woman 91

6: Crossing the Threshold of Hope. 135

7: Abandonment to Divine Providence 156

Introduction to the Catholic Classics

Opening Prayer

Lord, our Church is filled with the wisdom and knowledge of the saints. Guide us in being lifelong learners of their talents. Help us to glean from their work the specific ideas and practices you most desire for us, Lord. We seek always to do your will above all else and trust in the teaching power of our brothers and sisters who have gone before us, marked with the sign of faith. Increase our faith, hope, and trust in you, and in your Church. We ask this in the precious name of Jesus.

Amen.

The Classic Classics: A Bounty of Books and Saints

I am a cradle Catholic and a college librarian. I suppose, therefore, that it is my life's dream to be writing a Scripture study for women based on a body of classical literature formed by some of the best writers in our Church's history. That really makes it sound like I am a giant nerd, and you would be correct!

Nothing energizes me more than a good book. Curling up on the corner of the couch, a cup of tea by my side, I put on my glasses in the evening and pick up either the physical book I am currently reading or my Kindle e-reader. I love to escape into a story and to learn new things. Even the process of selecting a new book to read after I finish another one brings me great excitement! Should I try out a new genre or an author I have never read before? Perhaps delve into a different subject I have recently become passionate about? The possibilities are endless.

Therefore, preparing for this Scripture study was pure joy. Our faith is positively filled with the works of Doctors of the Church and other saintly writers, and many of them are cited commonly enough to be given the designation of "a Catholic classic." I have included some of them here, but, of course, it would take a lifetime to study all of them! I also included some more-modern works that I think have incredible relatability for contemporary women in the Church. I think that these newer works have a powerful message to share and are spiritual classics in the making. Any list of just seven books within the overwhelming bounty that make up the written body of our Church is going to involve quite a bit of discretion, and that is what I employed here. I hope that you are eager to see my list and study these spiritual gems along with me!

In this Scripture study, we will be opening our Bibles, as well as learning from the following authors and works:

- **Thomas á Kempis'** *The Imitation of Christ.* Thomas á Kempis teaches us about avoiding distraction, the importance of work and carrying our own cross, and the crucial nature of seeking out the Eucharist on a regular basis.

- **St. Thérèse of Lisieux's autobiography,** *The Story of a Soul.* St. Thérèse speaks to us about having a childlike faith and to relish our smallness before God, about being willing to accept suffering, and about how God loves us and calls us each to specific purposes.

- **St. Teresa of Avila's** *The Way of Perfection.* St. Teresa writes powerfully about detachment from material objects and humility, and offers fascinating tidbits of advice about prayer. St. Teresa was writing for her community of religious sisters, but her advice is indispensable in our homes, our domestic monasteries!

- **St. Francis de Sales'** *Introduction to the Devout Life.* Four hundred years before our time, St. Francis was writing for the twenty-first-century woman, and I think that he would be pleased that his missionary zeal to reach the everyday person was a success! He presents us with advice about courage, confession, interior peace amidst chaos, and battling anxiety. Can you see why I love him so much?

- **St. Teresa Benedicta of the Cross/Edith Stein's** *On Woman.* St. Edith is a modern woman after my own heart. Her work is akin to taking one of her college philosophy classes and learning from her about the unique nature of femininity and making the Eucharist the center of our lives.

↗ **St. John Paul II's** *Crossing the Threshold of Hope.* One of my favorite human beings of all time, and another philosopher, St. John Paul II tackles the big questions: faith, suffering, evangelization, and trust.

↗ **Fr. Jean-Pierre de Caussade's** *Abandonment to Divine Providence.* How could we end in any way other than learning how to abandon ourselves completely to God's will for our lives? Fr. de Caussade addresses this topic with vigor and, also, touches upon the roles of love, faith, and emotion.

From these holy men and women, we are presented with a wealth of spiritual riches. Their larger works are, of course, well worth reading, but what I have done here is to select six key passages to explore from each book. We will delve into those together and then relate them to pertinent Scripture selections to support us on our Christian walk. In this way, we are introduced to the writings of the saints in a way that is relatable to the lives of women living in the twenty-first century. I hope that you are as excited about this journey as I am!

Closing Prayer

Lord, thank you for being with us as we embark on a new journey. Bless our time together as we read through these spiritual books, and help us to learn as much as we can from them. Please prepare our hearts to be students again, sitting at the feet of our wise instructor, who loves us and wants to teach us with gentle compassion. Help us to absorb these lessons into our hearts for the betterment of our own souls and to spread them out far and wide into your kingdom. We ask all of this in the precious name of Jesus.

Amen.

1: The Imitation of Christ

Opening Prayer

Dear Lord, help us to read this classic work on Christian living so that we glean understanding about our own daily walk. How can we imitate Christ in our own lives whether we are religious or laywomen, married or single? In all of our differences we are united in the Body of Christ and in the Church, and therefore help us, Lord, to support each other in every one of our undertakings.

Each day when we wake, help us to greet the dawn with a renewed faith in you and a revitalized hope in our endeavors, both earthly and eternal. As we walk through our daily journey of prayer, work, and recreation, help us to see you in all things. We want to turn to you, Lord, for all of our needs and in all of our joys and sorrows. Be there with us, Lord, and place your hand on our shoulders. We endeavor always to love and please you more. We pray for the ability to follow the example of Thomas á Kempis in striving for holiness and in imitating the life of our Savior.

Guide us, Lord, as you instruct us in the Gospel of Luke 9:62, in never looking back after we have put our hand to the plow. We ask this in the precious name of Jesus. Amen.

On My Heart

_____

_____

_____

_____

_____

_____

_____

_____

_____

_____

_____

_____

_____

The Blessing of Thomas á Kempis

Thomas á Kempis, a fifteenth-century Augustinian monk, wrote *The Imitation of Christ* as a guide to the interior life. If you are like me, you may find classical works of spirituality to be heavy and difficult to understand. This book, however, while so thoroughly chock full of wisdom that a Christian could spend a lifetime meditating upon its passages, is remarkably easy to relate to one's own spiritual walk when examined bit by bit.

It is arranged as a series of four smaller books combined into one larger volume, addressing the following:

1. *Helpful Counsels for the Spiritual Life*
2. *Directives for the Interior Life*
3. *On Interior Consolation*
4. *On the Blessed Sacrament*

For Thomas á Kempis, these four things are integral to an intimate union with our Creator. I have chosen passages from each of the four books for us to study and apply in our own lives, which are likely quite different from that of a monk living in the fifteenth century. Nevertheless, I think that the message pervades time and state in life.

Reflection on Selections from *The Imitation of Christ*

> Much peace could be ours if we did not occupy ourselves with what others say and do, for such things are of no concern to us. How can we long to remain in peace if we involve ourselves in other people's business, if we seek outside distractions, and if we are rarely, or only to a small degree, interiorly recollected? Blessed are they who keep to themselves, for they shall enjoy much peace.[1]

As a laywoman, a woman living in the world rather than a member of a religious order, the first thought that comes to my mind when reading the above is the sin of gossip. If we are "involving ourselves in other people's business," perhaps we are commenting on things in a judgmental fashion or otherwise being nosy in an uncharitable way. It is easy to fall into this sin while justifying to ourselves that we are, in fact, innocent of it. This is a constant reminder that I must give to myself.

Relatedly, when we gossip, we are falling into the common predisposition to insecurity. Even after all of my own decades of life, I am still not immune to this struggle. When I am feeling insecure about something, I want to know what others are doing so that I can compare myself in a reassuring way. For example, I am a dancer, and despite my joy and happiness in this regard, it is very easy for me to devolve into petty anxiety and insecurity about how well my interpretation of the music stacks up against my peers. In reality, it should not matter what anyone else is doing. I have a passion for dancing, and if I put my best effort into my performance, that is all I need to be concerned with. When I give dancing all of my attention and energy, that, in and of itself, is enough. I can have peace in my own abilities, as they are what God gave to me. Indeed, there is such solace in not seeking outside distractions in the form of other people's business. Yet, often I am so stubbornly resistant in my approach to this!

Why do you seek rest when you were born to work? Prepare yourself for patient suffering rather than for consolation, for bearing the cross rather than for rejoicing. Who is the man in this world who would not gladly welcome spiritual joy and consolation if he could always have them?[2]

At first glance, this particular passage seems a bit harsh, yes? We were not born to rest, but to work, and we need to be prepared for "patient suffering, rather than for consolation." It is true that we must bear our crosses, but we will at times feel spiritual consolation. It may not come as emotional or physical consolation in the way we were hoping and praying for, but it will still soothe our souls and bring us joy. This will involve a shift in perspective for us: we cannot depend upon worldly happiness to bring satisfaction to our lives; we must rely solely on Christ because he knows exactly what we need.

As I go about my daily tasks that come from being a wife and mother, as well as an academic librarian working outside of the home, I find many opportunities for patient suffering! Exasperation is my constant companion, it seems. My children do not always listen or do what I ask them to do, nor do the students I teach, and the end result is frustrating for everyone involved. I am not going to always enjoy my daily responsibilities and tasks, but they are due my full effort and attention. God will send us the peace and solace we need when we need it.

Spiritual consolation surpasses all worldly delights and bodily pleasures. The delights of this world are worthless and vile, but those of the spirit are joyful and noble, for they alone proceed from virtuous deeds and are infused by God into a pure heart. No man can always enjoy divine consolation no matter how much he would like to—his time of temptation has not yet come to an end.[3]

And so, we are going about our daily work with patient suffering, and the other side of this issue is that God will console us. Although in our human nature we mourn the difficulties we face each day and any losses that we must bear, spiritual consolations will ultimately come our way and should surpass our worldly feelings. This is not an easy passage for me to put into practice, I must admit. When Thomas á Kempis says that the delights of the world are "worthless and vile," my first reaction is one of disquiet. My sense, though, is that he is putting emphasis on the fact that we need to let go of our attachment to these things. The people in our lives and the hobbies we enjoy are in and of themselves a blessing, but we must be wary of our attachment to them superseding our relationship with God and our ultimate goal of heaven. We, indeed, live in a time of temptation—so many challenges come up in our daily lives that prove this. We may not always feel the consolation of God, but that does not change the fact that he is always there.

Jesus [speaking to the author]: You must conform all your desires to My good pleasure and stop loving yourself, and earnestly desire that My will be done. You frequently burn with desires that powerfully impel you to action, but what is the motive behind your actions? Is it My honor or is it your own self-interest? If I be the motive, then you will be satisfied with whatever I decide for you; but if it be your own self-interest, then this is what puts the brake to your progress and slows you down.[4]

I am sighing very heavily as I read this particular passage; is anyone else joining me? This message relates as much to my confused journey of seeking and discovering in my twenties as it does now to my harried vocation as a wife and mother nearly twenty years later. (By vocation, I am referring to one's ultimate calling in state of life, whether that be to the religious, married, or single life.) Indeed, what are my motives when I make decisions in my role as a wife and mom? If I am being honest, too often I do not consult the Lord in prayer, but simply go forward with what I believe is best at that moment. Has this ever gone poorly? you rightly ask.

Why yes, yes it has. We all need to make that time for prayerful discernment, that is, for listening to God's voice in our lives and seeking his will, even when bad days at work and crying babies are dominating our thoughts. As much as I love God, I still rely very much on myself, especially when I am experiencing worry and anxiety about some large life event. I know this about myself, and I continue to work on it daily. There are some lessons that I believe are more difficult than others for us to take to heart and apply in our own lives!

Therefore, be careful not to rely too heavily on your own desires without first consulting Me. You may later on find that you are sorry and displeased with what once pleased you and what you once thought the better thing to do.[5]

Our perspective and feelings on things do change over time, do they not? I cringe when I reflect back on some decisions I made earlier in my life, thinking at the time that it was what I wanted. I suppose it was, in fact, what I wanted, but did I once think about consulting God first? I did not. And in the end, the result did not actually make me happy. If there is anything I have learned as the years have passed, it is that waiting is very often the right call. Taking time to consult God and then waiting to hear his voice is crucial. If, after the short waiting period, you still feel quite conflicted, the answer may be no. I do not like to be told no, but I have tried to accept it more as I have gotten older.

"You may later on find that you are sorry and displeased with what once pleased you..." Truer words have never been spoken, correct? Although I have learned some lessons in my lifetime, this one is still a struggle for me, despite the painful manner in which certain situations have resolved in the past when I tried to do things by myself!

Some people refrain from going to Holy Communion because of an undue concern whether they are sufficiently devout, or because of some anxiety about going to confession. In this matter, follow the counsel of someone who is wise and banish all anxiety and scruple, for such thinking is a hindrance to God's grace and it destroys whatever devotion is in the soul. Don't give up receiving Holy Communion because of some trivial matter or trifling annoyance, but quickly go and confess it, and gladly forgive all who have offended you. And if you have offended anyone, then humbly ask God's pardon and He will generously forgive you.[6]

Thomas á Kempis devotes an entire book to the Eucharist, which demonstrates the central importance he places on it in the context of our faith. I especially enjoy how he weaves in the ever common avoidance of confession as something we need to overcome in order to more fully envelop the Eucharist into our lives. Have I ever avoided confession due to anxiety or "undue concern whether [I] am sufficiently devout"? One thousand times, yes! In fact, it happens nearly every single time I think about availing myself of this particular sacrament. Yet, if we are not regularly seeking out the sacrament of Reconciliation, we are unlikely to be in the proper condition to receive the Eucharist, which is what this passage is warning us against.

No matter what is happening in our own lives at any given time, we need the Eucharist. Confession is a conduit for making this happen, and we should not let it intimidate us and keep us from the One we love.

Conclusion

Thomas á Kempis has a lot to share with us about the Christian walk, and we are barely brushing the surface with the passages I have selected! I think, though, that we can draw some important lessons from his words, as well as from the related Scripture verses.

The first is that we should do our best to allow our minds to rest easy in God's good and loving care, and to avoid being distracted by our own fears and the goings on of others. I am attempting to picture this idyllic version of me, able to eschew all worldly distractions and failing miserably! It is, however, what we are called to do each and every day as followers of Jesus. We may not always succeed, but putting our hand to the plow and then never looking back is always our goal.

Secondly, our lives are intended for hard work and spiritual, rather than worldly, consolation. We are not guaranteed to have earthly happiness, that is for certain. Although at first glance this teaching seems mildly disheartening, it is important to remember that God always knows what is best for us. His consolation will ultimately make us so much happier than the comforts of the world ever could. It is an interior solace and peace that is the vital balm for our souls.

Thirdly, and relatedly, we are called to carry our cross and, thus, grow in a desire to see God's will, rather than our own, be done. It is very difficult, in my experience, to move away from the mindset of how I want things done. When I correct my children as they attempt to complete a task around the house, it's always because they are not doing so in the manner that I would complete the task myself had I not asked them to do it. I notice myself adopting this attitude toward God in prayer as well! I have a very specific idea of how I, ideally, would like things to go, and that is that. I may tell God that I am open to his will being done, but I do not actually mean it. I am constantly asking myself how I can truly and genuinely mean it when I pray for God's will to be done in my life.

Finally, and toward this end of endeavoring to always be open to God's will, we should seek out the Eucharist as often as we can. It is a genuine leap of faith to accept that the Eucharist is the literal body and blood of our Lord. It is an instrument powerful enough to make us change our lives. Could other people discern, based on the way we live our lives, that we believe that our Savior dwells among us in this way?

Together, we must eschew worldly distractions, bravely carry our cross, always seek God's will, confess our sins, and receive the Eucharist regularly. None of these things are what I would term easy, yet our Lord asks them of us and has confidence that we are up to the task.

An Invitation to Ponder

Do I always consult God before making decisions, both large and small? If not, in what ways can I remind myself about this important step in the future (for example, carry a holy card in my wallet, keep a rosary in my car, etc.)? In what ways can I structure a prayer routine that will help me to focus on Jesus and the cross as I go about the other daily tasks of my work?

_____

_____

_____

_____

_____

_____

_____

_____

_____

_____

_____

_____

_____

_____

_____

Connecting to Scripture

Take time to read each Scripture passage referenced below (and in each of the subsequent chapters), and pay special attention to what the Holy Spirit is calling your attention to in each verse. Do not concern yourself with right or wrong responses; simply relax and allow yourself to truly enjoy this time with the Word of God. Be assured, Jesus has no expectations for your time together; there is no perfect rubric for your time with Jesus, whether you are in prayer, reading Scriptures, or participating in the sacraments. The beauty of the *Stay Connected Journals for Catholic Women* series[7] is that the time you spend with these books is your prayer time. Each of these journals is designed to be a guide for a personal encounter with the Triune God—Father, Son, and Holy Spirit.

If you wish, read each verse a few times, asking the Holy Spirit to guide your heart and mind to receive what he has prepared just for you. Use the space provided under each Scripture verse to note any inspirations or thoughts that come to you as you read. Share your thoughts with a small group or maintain your notes as a personal reflection.

PRAYER TO THE HOLY SPIRIT BEFORE READING SCRIPTURE

Come, Holy Spirit. Guide me in receiving the message, lovingly personalized just for me, awaiting me here in God's Word. Open my heart to understand and accept what the Scriptures can teach me today. Amen.

🖙 Job 5:6-9 _____

_____

_____

🖙 Matthew 6:9-14 _____

_____

_____

🖙 Matthew 16:24-28 _____

_____

_____

✐ Mark 11:22-26 _____

_____

_____

✐ Luke 9:61-62 _____

_____

_____

✐ John 6:67-69 _____

_____

_____

Scripture Reflection

I sat down to read my Bible one evening after the kids had gone to bed, and I read in the Gospel of Luke 9:62 how Jesus told a prospective disciple, "No one who sets a hand to the plow and looks to what was left behind is fit for the kingdom of God." I felt myself gulp rather dramatically. Does this scenario sound familiar to anyone else?

Luke 9:61-62 is a very intense verse. In our everyday lives as women, I am certain that many, or even most, of us feel overwhelmed by our tasks, and our focus is all over the place. Yet, giving these things all of our singular focus, rather than gazing firmly on Christ, is not what we are called to do. As women, we take our work very seriously, but we must remember that we can do nothing without him. Being "interiorly recollected," as Thomas á Kempis describes, should be our daily goal, even if many days it seems unattainable!

Inevitably, difficult days will come our way. Who better to be our guide in patient suffering than Job? Thomas á Kempis cites this specific verse from the book of Job 5:6–9, and I pondered it for a few moments before understanding what he was trying to show us. We become very easily distracted by worldly concerns, but our focus should always fixate on the cross. It is not good for our minds to become mired in the affairs of the world. Our God-given earthly work aids us in keeping our minds rooted in the foundation that is the spiritual life. In the end, importantly, God is good and, as Job describes in 5:9, does "things great and unsearchable, things marvelous and innumerable." Our trust in him should not fail.

Managing daily struggles without a tangible feeling of God's presence or consolation is no easy task. Indeed, Jesus, himself, instructs us in Matthew 16:24, "Whoever wishes to come after me must deny himself, take up his cross, and follow me." This is our command, we know that we must do this, but it does not always come naturally to us. As women, we oftentimes place the needs of numerous other people ahead of ourselves. And now we are supposed to place yet another thing ahead of our own needs? Yes, God wants us to take care of ourselves, certainly, but at the root of our existence is the fact that we are called to take up the daily crosses of suffering that are sent our way. We may not always know how these challenges will turn out, but we must trust that God has a larger plan for all of them.

What better way to listen for God's voice than to call to mind his very words, the Lord's Prayer in Matthew 6:9–14? I know that I often recite this prayer in a rote fashion, without really thinking about the words.

Pause over each and every word, and your experience with the Lord's Prayer will be transformed.

Embracing suffering does not sound abundantly appealing, to be sure, but God will only call us to things that are for our good. "Your kingdom come, your will be done, on earth as in heaven." Remember how Thomas á Kempis suggests we examine our motives to determine whether we are pursuing our own plans rather than God's? "If I be the motive, then you will be satisfied with whatever I decide for you; but if it be your own self-interest, then this is what puts the brake to your progress and slows you down."[8] Although our plans may originally head in a different direction than where they end up, we should endeavor to be open to this being God's will for our lives. God doesn't just rule in heaven; he rules on earth as well. For our part, though, we must accept his invitation into our earthly lives. We have free will. Thus, we can reject his will, and perhaps in a weak moment, this may seem like a desirable and good idea.

In the end, however, our happiness rests with our Creator. We can pursue what we believe will make us happy without consulting God, but we will never be as fully and completely satiated as we will when we first seek him before making decisions.

Acceptance, though, requires faith—faith that one will be able to work through the situation regardless of the result, and faith in God's goodness above all else. In Mark 11:22–23, Jesus tells us, "Have faith in God. Amen, I say to you, whoever says to this mountain, 'Be lifted up and thrown into the sea,' and does not doubt in his heart but believes that what he says will happen, it shall be done for him." If a situation ends tragically, it is very easy to doubt God's love and mercy. In these times, we must have faith, even if we feel that we are faithfully accepting the result as a sheer act of the will. This will inevitably happen to all of us at some point, and God does not mind if we are a bit angry in our faith. His shoulders are strong enough to take our anger. Our job is simply to persevere in faith.

The Eucharist, of course, is the summit of our faith. I have made some poor choices in my life, and I shudder when I think back on them, despite having sought forgiveness, and received absolution via the sacrament of Reconciliation. I think back on how I had avoided attending Mass during those portions of my life. Thomas á Kempis encourages us to never avoid the Eucharist "because of an undue concern whether they are sufficiently devout, or because of some anxiety about going to confession."[9] Does this apply to you? I am betting that at some point in your life it applied, or applies, to everyone! Our author is directing us to never let this anxiety take hold because the Eucharist is so incredibly central to the blossoming of our faith. And the Eucharist, of course, is Jesus.

Indeed, we see the following in John 6:67–68: "'Do you also want to leave?' Simon Peter answered him, 'Master, to whom shall we go? You have the words of eternal life.'" This may be my favorite verse in the entire Bible. We live in a very large and complicated world. Our global Church has a lot of rituals and doctrines for us to learn. In the end, however, it all comes down to Jesus. And Jesus is in the Eucharist. Are our lives reflecting that essential fact?

An Invitation to Share

1. What are the different ways in which Thomas á Kempis, although far removed from the life experience of the members of this Bible study, is relatable to a twenty-first-century woman?

_____

_____

_____

_____

_____

_____

_____

_____

2. Faithfulness. Trust. Discipleship. In what ways has Thomas á Kempis challenged your views or the views of the group on these issues?

_____

_____

_____

_____

_____

_____

_____

_____

_____

_____

_____

3. Thomas á Kempis speaks a lot about prayer. How do his words on speaking with our Lord in prayer compare with how you or members of the group have viewed prayer in the past?

_____

_____

_____

_____

_____

_____

_____

_____

4. Who are some other important saints who have spoken about the centrality of the Eucharist in the Catholic faith? How did this impact their daily walk as Christians?

_____

_____

_____

_____

_____

_____

_____

_____

Closing Prayer

Dear Lord, thank you for calling us together to study your Word and the work of Thomas á Kempis. Help us to strive for holiness with the fervor that he has shown us in his writing.

Lord, we want so much to do your will, but so often we fail, according to our own hopes and expectations. Give us the strength to be earnest in our efforts to abandon ourselves to your will. We pray that our daily crosses bring us closer to you, and to each other, in faith, hope, and love. Guide us as we discern decisions in our lives together, Lord. Fortify us so that we may guard ourselves against worldly distractions and seek your holy face. We ask this in the precious name of Jesus.

Amen.

2: The Story of a Soul

Opening Prayer

Dear Lord, help us to emulate St. Thérèse of Lisieux, who always strove for childlike holiness and confidence in you. St. Thérèse exemplified the "little way" of holiness in her daily activities: cleaning, praying, and interacting with her sisters. In each small movement of her day, she saw an opportunity to give you glory. Our lives, too, are filled with mundane, albeit meaningful, tasks: daily responsibilities at our jobs, cleaning our homes, and taking care of the needs of our family and friends. Each one of these things, though seemingly unrelated to our eternal souls, is, in fact, part of our spiritual journey. Please help us to always remember this and to perform all of these tasks with great love.

Although St. Thérèse's life in a Carmelite monastery was very different from our own, her example permeates all walks of life. We pray that we will think of her and her example often as we work throughout our days. St. Thérèse, please pray for us to love God more!

Guide us, Lord, in striving to be holy in the tiniest of endeavors, just like St. Thérèse. We ask this in the precious name of Jesus. Amen.

On My Heart

_____

_____

_____

_____

_____

_____

_____

_____

_____

_____

_____

_____

_____

The Blessing of St Thérèse of Lisieux

I have heard St. Thérèse of Lisieux referred to as a person with whom it is difficult to relate. In her case, we have a young French woman, who, as a child, described herself as quite spoiled. She later experienced a religious awakening that led her to pursue a cloistered Carmelite vocation as a teenager. As a cloistered sister, St. Thérèse lived in a monastery with a community of other women, physically enclosed and separated from the world. With fewer young men and women pursuing vocations to the religious life in our contemporary time, as opposed to when St. Thérèse was alive in the late nineteenth century, her decision at age fifteen to enter a monastery may be quite shocking. She even had to seek the permission of the pope, himself, to join the Carmelites because of her young age!

I, personally, feel quite the opposite, however. Although my life to this point has been quite different from the one St. Thérèse lived, I find her personality, her innermost being, as related to us in her autobiography, quite relatable to this twenty-first-century wife and mother. As we reflect on passages from her life story, I think that you will see what I mean.

Reflection on Selections from *Story of a Soul*

At the very outset of *Story of a Soul,* St. Thérèse tells us:

> Before starting, I knelt before the statue of Mary, the one which has given us so many proofs that the Queen of heaven looks after us like a mother. I begged her to guide my hand so that I should not write a line that would displease her. Then I opened the Gospels and saw these words: 'Then he went up onto the mountainside, and called to him those whom it pleased him to call.' There, indeed, was the mystery of my vocation, of my whole life, and of the special graces given me by Jesus. He does not call those who are worthy, but those he chooses.[10]

A call. Do we not *all* wonder about this at some point? St. Thérèse, being in her twenties as she writes these words, represents a time in life during which we each wonder what we are called to do. The large questions are certainly on all of our minds at that point in our journey. I recall, quite vividly, being twenty-four years old, freshly out of graduate school, and feeling rather uncertain about what would come next. I was not exactly in love with my job, and Mr. Right had not yet found me, given that I was quietly hiding out in my parents' house and attempting to pay off my student loan debt. St. Thérèse points out, quite rightly, that our work in whatever we are ultimately called to do, is not based on our worthiness. It is because God chose it for us. Indeed, he chose *us*. We may not feel worthy, but that does not diminish the importance of our call.

Every Lent, I think back on this sentiment anew. I set up spiritual goals for myself, but, inevitably, I will not have followed through on all, or even most, of them by the time Easter approaches. I feel this exact sense of unworthiness that St. Thérèse speaks of. How can I do great things for God if I cannot even keep my promise of a daily Rosary for Lent? Her reminder is right on point: Jesus does not call those who are worthy. That is where our focus should lie.

He set the book of nature before me and I saw that all the flow-ers he has created are lovely. The splendor of the rose and the whiteness of the lily do not rob the little violet of its scent nor the daisy of its simple charm. I realized that if every tiny flower wanted to be a rose, spring would lose its loveliness and there would be no wildflowers to make the meadows gay. It is just the same in the world of souls—which is the garden of Jesus. he has created the great saints who are like the lilies and the roses, but he has also created much lesser saints and they must be content to be the daisies or the violets which rejoice His eyes whenever he glances down. Perfection consists in doing His will, in being that which he wants us to be.[11]

St. Thérèse's garden analogy really touches my heart. Some are called to be great and beautiful roses, but many of us are called to be small, albeit still lovely, daisies. All of us have a place in Jesus' garden. We do not need to compare ourselves to those whom we deem greater than ourselves. God has called us to fill a specific role, and we should cherish that role, as it is quite needed in his garden.

Although St. Thérèse's calling was much different from mine, I still find her process of discovering her role in God's plan to be very relatable to my own struggles. Like St. Thérèse, I feel quite small and unimportant in the larger world. I know that my family and friends love and appreciate me, as I do them, but in the grander view of the universe, I see myself as very small. Even in our smallness, though, God can still use us.

God would not make me wish for something impossible, and so, in spite of my littleness, I can aim at being a saint. It is impossible for me to grow bigger, so I put up with myself as I am, with all of my countless faults. But I will look for some means of going to heaven by a little way which is very short and very straight, a little way that is quite new. We live in an age of inventions. We need no longer climb laboriously up flights of stairs; in well-to-do houses there are lifts. And I was determined to find a lift to carry me to Jesus, for I was far too small to climb the steep stairs of perfection. So I sought in Holy Scripture some idea of what this lift I wanted would be, and I read these words from the mouth of eternal Wisdom: 'Whosoever is a little one, let him come to me.' I drew nearer to God, fully realizing that I had found what I was looking for.[12]

This is what St. Thérèse is most known for, the "little way" of holiness. She describes herself as being like a little child before her Savior, always, even when she was a grown woman. Indeed, all of us are God's children, and we can rely on and trust him in this important, childlike way. As well, St. Thérèse spoke of offering up to God little tasks and challenges throughout her day, as small ways of pleasing him and growing in our own ability to sacrifice for others and toward obedience. Living in a community of other women in close quarters, her opportunities for such offering up were plentiful. For us, in our day jobs and family relationships, in changing diapers and washing dishes, the same is true.

As an academic librarian, I do a lot of teaching. The day-to-day reality of this routine is that I encounter a lot of things that try my patience: students who are rude, students who do not complete their work yet still want a good grade, technology not working properly at the worst possible moment, the list could go on and on. However, I often think of St. Thérèse when I encounter these scenarios. I can offer up these frustrations like she did, as an opportunity to allow peace back into my mind and to grow in my obedience to God. The alternative is to give in to tears, and I prefer St. Thérèse's method!

I also wanted to know how God would deal with a 'little one,' so I continued my search and found this: 'you shall be carried at the breasts and upon the knees; as one whom the mother caresseth, so will I comfort you.' Never before had I been gladdened by such sweet and tender words. It is your arms, Jesus, which are the lift to carry me to heaven. And there is no need for me to grow up. In fact, just the opposite: I must stay little and become less and less.[13]

This image of motherhood that St. Thérèse paints here melts my heart. I think about holding a baby, my own or someone else's, and I always gaze down at their little faces and reflect on the sweetness that lies there, on how every little thing that they do—a tiny sneeze or a trusting grasp of our finger in their small fist—is infinitely precious. This verse from St. Thérèse reminds me that our Lord sees us in this tender fashion. Although we are going to make mistakes every day, Jesus still sees the sweetness in us. His gaze is still that of a parent: loving fondness beyond all measure.

Her description of Jesus' arms being "the lift" to get us to heaven makes me smile. I now think of Jesus' arms as an elevator of sorts, lifting us up to our heavenly home. Our trust is what gives rise to the apparatus.

Though I'm quite unworthy, I love to say the Divine Office every day, but apart from that I cannot bring myself to hunt through books for beautiful prayers. There are so many of them that I get a headache. Besides, each prayer seems lovelier than the next. I cannot possibly say them all and do not know which to choose, I behave like children who cannot read: I tell God very simply what I want and he always understands. For me, prayer is an upward leap of the heart, an untroubled glance towards heaven, a cry of gratitude and love which I utter from the depths of sorrow as well as from the heights of joy. It has a supernatural grandeur which expands the soul and unites it with God. I say an Our Father or a Hail Mary when I feel so spiritually barren that I cannot summon up a single worthwhile thought. These two prayers fill me with rapture and feed and satisfy my soul. [14]

I love and chose this verse from St. Thérèse's autobiography because it shows how very human and insecure she was—just like the rest of us! Prayer is befuddling even to a young woman who became a nun at age fifteen. Let us talk for a few moments about prayer in general and about what St. Thérèse teaches us about it here.

When she speaks of the Divine Office, this is the Liturgy of the Hours, the official prayer of the Church that priests are obliged to pray every single day. The prayers of the Liturgy of the Hours, which traditionally come in a four-volume set of books, originate in the Psalms and elsewhere in Scripture and are divided up over the Church calendar for special feast days and the liturgical seasons of Advent/Christmas and Lent/Easter. It is a beautiful system for prayer wherein a person prays seven times throughout the day to mark the passage of time. Laypeople and other religious may also pray the Liturgy of the Hours though it is not mandatory and for laypeople it is not common. Most of the time, laypeople, like you and I, pray traditional prayers we learned early in our faith formation, such as the Our Father and Hail Mary, or we simply speak with God in the silence of our hearts and minds.

I sometimes come across beautiful prayers on the backs of holy cards or find verses in Scripture that I meditate on, and, of course, all of these are excellent methods of praying. St. Thérèse brings home the crux of the issue: we could easily dissuade ourselves from praying and become overwhelmed if we make the process too complicated. Indeed, what is complicated to one person may not be for another, this will differ greatly across individual states in life and preferences. In other words, the important thing is to simply *pray*. In whatever way is most natural to you on a given day, in a specific moment, simply do that. God always understands what we are trying to say to him.

But now I am ill and I shall not get better. Yet I am at peace. For a long time I have not belonged to myself, but have completely abandoned myself to Jesus...So he is free to do whatever he wants with me. he gave the desire for exile and asked if I would drink from that chalice. I tried at once to grasp it, but he withdrew it, satisfied with my willingness.[15]

St. Thérèse died of tuberculosis at just twenty-four years old. Her death was painful and drawn out. Although she had moments of doubt in her faith, she did not despair. I truly admire her abandonment to God, even in the depths of her suffering. Granted, I do not think that I am alone in feeling that I do reach out to God more when I am going through a crisis than when life is going swimmingly. A crisis can take any number of forms, but for St. Thérèse it was quite extreme—that she had contracted a fatal illness. That level of suffering requires a whole new measure of trust, in my mind. Even amidst her physical struggles at this time in her life, she still felt God lifting her up. She "tried at once to grasp" the cup of suffering that he offered her, but "he withdrew it, satisfied with my willingness." Despite her disease, she felt true consolation in her reward to come. This earthly illness could not diminish her desire for that union with her Savior, the comfort of that knowledge. Her spirit was willing to endure this trial so that she could be with Jesus.

I find St. Thérèse to be a woman of great compassion and mercy. I do not often see myself as childlike at this stage of my life, yet I want to emulate St. Thérèse and her daily road to holiness. St. Thérèse's vision does harken childlike joy into my faith and into my worldview. I love that God gave us her example to learn from.

Conclusion

St. Thérèse presents us with a unique approach to our interior faith lives. Interestingly, she is the patron saint of missionaries, though she never traveled abroad. The reason is that she dedicated her life as a Carmelite to praying for missionaries and their efforts. Indeed, St. Thérèse has a lot to teach us about our prayer lives and our relationship with God. She has a lot to offer regarding the interior life. Let us look at the main points we gleaned from her in this study.

St. Thérèse speaks to us of being called and how God chooses whom he calls. In fact, our calling is not based on our worthiness. Those of us who feel that drawn to God are chosen simply because he loves us. Indeed, each of us has something different to offer to God and to others. St. Thérèse shows us with her beautiful garden analogy how all flowers are important in God's garden. We may be small flowers while others are bright and beautiful roses, but that does not diminish our usefulness. God wants each of us for a different purpose.

Smallness is a large theme within St. Thérèse's model of spirituality. She speaks a lot about being childlike in our approach to God. Even as a grown woman, St. Thérèse felt this role before God in a very poignant way. She had very adult responsibilities in her daily life, as we all do, but when she spoke to her Father, she was like a child. Indeed, God does ask this of us because it keeps our minds and hearts humble. When we pray, we can imitate St. Thérèse and remember to keep simplicity in our prayer. That may mean different approaches for different individuals, which is the way it should be. God made us all different. Some days our spirits may long to meditate on the Psalms and other Scripture verses, but other days we may barely be able to remember the words to the Our Father.

As she went about her day-to-day tasks, St. Thérèse always thought about a lift to carry her to Jesus because steep stairs would be too overwhelming for someone who saw herself as so small. She wanted a little way that was short and straight, a way that she could realistically follow to grow in holiness within her place and station in life. This "little way of holiness" is what she is most known for. As she scrubbed floors in the convent, kept silent when dealing with a particularly curmudgeonly sister, and washed dishes, she offered these actions and sacrifices of spirit up to God. For me, this is the most relatable part of St. Thérèse's approach to the spiritual life. We all have to do things on a daily basis that we would rather not do: tasks at work, particularly-stinky diapers to change, or gigantic messes (physical or otherwise) created by other people to clean up. We do these things, but they can have greater meaning by offering them to God. When we do them in this spirit of charity, it can transform us.

Finally, St. Thérèse is an example of willingness to accept suffering. She did not have an easy time of things, being such a young woman in a heavily structured environment like a Carmelite convent and then suffering from such a painful, fatal illness. Yet she accepted these things as God's will for her life. She still struggled amongst these things, to be sure, as any of us would. Her spirit, however, was ultimately willing. That is indeed what we should all strive for.

An Invitation to Ponder

Do I allow feelings of unworthiness to bring me to despair, to not continue to strive to improve myself? If so, in what way can I remind myself daily that God has chosen me and wants me for himself? What do I do on a daily basis that shows how I have chosen God?

Connecting to Scripture

PRAYER TO THE HOLY SPIRIT BEFORE READING SCRIPTURE

Come, Holy Spirit. Guide me in receiving the message, lovingly personalized just for me, awaiting me here in God's Word. Open my heart to understand and accept what the Scriptures can teach me today. Amen.

✐ Proverbs 9:4-6 _____

_____

_____

✐ Isaiah 66:12-13 _____

_____

_____

✐ Matthew 6:5-8 _____

_____

_____

✐ Matthew 6:25-34 _____

_____

_____

✐ Matthew 18:1-5 _____

_____

_____

⑦ Mark 3:13–14 _____

_____

_____

Scripture Reflection

I love the translation of Mark 3:13 in my Bible, which says Jesus "summoned those whom he wanted." St. Thérèse spoke of this verse as God choosing us, and I also like this other wording of us being whom God wanted. He chose us; he wants us, even in our unworthiness. In the back of my mind, I know that this is a verse that I will need to come back to again and again throughout my life. No matter how many times I read it, it is very difficult for me to truly take it to heart. I keep letting God down; I keep failing. I sometimes make poor or insensitive choices. Of course, God wants us to strive to do better. Despite all that, he still wants us.

In Matthew 6:25–34, we are encouraged to be dependent upon God, to trust him. Our worrying shows a lack of trust in God's infinite gaze and care. And Jesus speaks to us about this using the analogy of a garden, replete with birdsong. We are but one small flower in God's beautiful garden, and this imagery really spoke to St. Thérèse. She repeatedly comes back to the point that our smallness is, in fact, a precious thing to our Lord.

Perhaps because I see myself as small and somewhat insignificant, I am a champion worrier. Worrying is almost a form of exercise for my mind, a way to make myself believe that I am doing something productive, rather than feeling helpless in the face of a situation over which I have no control. That, of course, is a fallacy. We may be small, but God still understands our worries and will take care of us. No flower is too small to escape his notice.

In Proverbs 9:4-6, we return to this notion of our smallness before God and how this does not mean that we lack importance or purpose. We still have a place in this world, and the next. There's certainly an eternal comfort to this knowledge that can carry us through our day-to-day tasks. I love St. Thérèse's take on this passage from Proverbs, when she says, "I drew nearer to God, fully realizing that I had found what I was looking for." We know that we are made in God's image, that he created us and wants us for himself. He chose us. Also important, though, is that we choose him. Every day, we can think of him and bask in the comfort of this love and acceptance of us. People often let us down, or say something to hurt us. God will never do this. In our smallness, we choose him and the absolute comfort that this brings.

Isaiah 66:13 shows us how much God always wants to comfort us: "As a mother comforts her child, so I will comfort you." I think of this often when I decide that it is time to seek out the sacrament of Reconciliation. Inevitably, I postpone this endeavor several times before I actually attend. The reason is that I am always in fear of offending God, of being ashamed of my continued failures. In the end, though, Jesus just wants to comfort us, to forgive us. We do not need to fear him.

In Matthew 6:5-8, we are told that God, our Father, sees our prayers to him, even when we are hidden away, and he knows exactly what we need before we ask him. St. Thérèse knew this, of course: "I tell God very simply what I want and he always understands." I often worry after I pray that my requests do not make any sense or that I forgot to mention something. It is ridiculous to worry about such things in the face of our omnipresent God, yet my own human insecurity trips me up every single time. St. Thérèse suffered from insecurity as well, in that she was not capable of choosing from amongst the vast array of beautiful prayers available to her. It is a wealth of riches in our faith, to be sure. She knew, though, that our exact words do not matter when we pray. Our Father knows what we need before we even sit down before him. Our childlike trust, our humbly coming before him, that is what brings us closer to him.

Indeed, Jesus tells us that unless we become like small children, we will not enter the kingdom of heaven, as he describes in Matthew 18:1–5. He specifically emphasizes the humility that children naturally possess, and that we need to humble ourselves before our God. Practicing humility is never an easy thing. My first reaction when I have made what turns out to have been a poor choice is to become defensive. Before God, though, there are no secrets with regard to our motivations or intentions. He knows, and he understands. Therefore, we must approach him with the humility that this loving, supportive relationship demands. St. Thérèse mentions how Jesus was satisfied with her willingness. That is what he is asking of us: our willingness to be humble before him.

An Invitation to Share

1. What are some ways in which we can hear God's voice in our own lives? In what ways can we discover what God is calling us to do?

_____

_____

_____

_____

_____

_____

_____

_____

_____

_____

_____

2. How is St. Thérèse's "little way of holiness" applicable to modern women in their secular jobs or in their responsibilities at home?

_____

_____

_____

_____

_____

_____

_____

_____

_____

_____

_____

3. What is one way that, as adult women, we can still see ourselves as childlike before our Savior?

_____

_____

_____

_____

_____

_____

_____

_____

4. In what ways is St. Thérèse's experience as a nun in the nineteenth century comparable to our secular lives in the twenty-first century?

_____

_____

_____

_____

_____

_____

_____

_____

_____

Closing Prayer

Dear Lord, thank you for calling us together to study your Word and the work of St. Thérèse of Lisieux. Help us to strive for holiness with the childlike faith and trust she has taught us about in her writing.

Lord, in all of our responsibilities and daily hardships, help us to imitate St. Thérèse. Her "little way of holiness" is an example for all of us, even those of us who have never felt a call to the religious life the way that she did. In our roles as women, caregivers, colleagues, family members, partners, and friends, we endeavor to seek your face with the innocent and trusting countenance of St. Thérèse. By her example, we pray that we will always do your will. We ask this in the precious name of Jesus.

Amen.

3: The Way of Perfection

Opening Prayer

Dear Lord, guide us in learning from the example of the great St. Teresa of Avila. In our lives as twenty-first-century women, in our jobs and relationships, in our roles as caregivers, help us to imitate the holy focus she provided to her Carmelite sisters: love, detachment from material things, and humility. Show us how to abandon ourselves to prayer the way that St. Teresa taught and to become absorbed in contemplating your sacrifice for us. Grant us the gift of concentration in our prayer, dear Lord.

As we go about our day-to-day responsibilities, help us to remember to pray unceasingly and to look for your hand everywhere. We endeavor to persevere, like St. Teresa, in our prayer for your will in our lives and in those of our loved ones. We aim to put our trust, not in material objects, but solely in your love for us.

Thank you, Lord, for giving us great saints like St. Teresa, who provides us with such a beautiful example. May her writings inspire us and generations to come. We ask this in the precious name of Jesus. Amen.

_____
_____
_____
_____
_____
_____
_____
_____
_____
_____
_____
_____
_____

The Blessing of St. Teresa of Avila

St. Teresa of Avila lived in Spain in the sixteenth century. She is best known for her reform of the Carmelite Order, now called the Discalced Carmelites for their propensity to be barefoot and humble before the Lord. St. Teresa left us with a large volume of writings on the spiritual life, which earned her the title of Doctor of the Church. *The Way of Perfection* is one of her most well-known pieces, and it is directed toward her Carmelite sisters living in cloistered monasteries. That being the case, her work, explaining interior and exterior holiness, is applicable to us all.

In *The Way of Perfection,* St. Teresa focuses on four main themes:

> *⒐ Fraternal love*
> *⒐ Detachment from material things*
> *⒐ True humility*
> *⒐ Prayer and contemplation*

We will focus here specifically on the latter three items and how these are very relevant to our lives as women over four hundred years removed from St. Teresa. Her vision for personal holiness transcends time.

Reflection on Selections from *The Way of Perfection*

> It will be a great help towards this if we keep constantly in our thoughts the vanity of all things and the rapidity with which they pass away, so that we may withdraw our affections from things which are so trivial and fix them upon what will never come to an end. This may seem a poor kind of help but it will have the effect of greatly fortifying the soul. With regard to small things, we must be very careful, as soon as we begin to grow fond of them, to withdraw our thoughts from them and turn them to God. His Majesty will help us to do this. He has granted us the great favour of providing that, in this house, most of it is done already; but it remains for us to become detached from our own selves and it is a hard thing to withdraw from ourselves and oppose ourselves, because we are very close to ourselves and love ourselves very dearly.[16]

St. Teresa starts us out with a difficult task, does she not? Detachment from our things, and even from ourselves, and directing our focus on the Lord is no easy goal. Unlike St. Teresa, we live in the secular world, and we are very reliant on material items in our lives to get us to and from our jobs, and for our households to run smoothly. Those items help us, it is true, and they are good in that way. I think St. Teresa's larger point, though, is our attachment to them. Allowing ourselves to become absorbed in acquiring new things and allowing our focus to linger on our pride in our possessions is where the problem comes in. We should not allow an emotional investment in our material goods to overtake our firm gaze on the Giver of these gifts.

As women, we are often in the role of caring for others. Whether it be caring for our children, our parents, our spouses, or another loved one, our nurturing nature often places us in these situations. During these times, we are so keenly aware of how we must withdraw from ourselves because someone else is relying so heavily on us for their own needs. We all, at times, need a reprieve from this type of intense detachment, to recharge and refresh. That is, indeed, the only sustainable way to carry on in a caregiving capacity for any length of time. The goal, though, is to recharge so as to be able to give fully of ourselves again. It is a good and healthy thing to take time to focus on our own wellness. We must always balance that time, however, with a spirit of detachment from our own desires for the betterment of others and prioritize our relationship with Jesus.

It is here that true humility can enter, for this virtue and that of detachment from self, I think, always go together. They are two sisters, who are inseparable. These are not the kinsfolk whom I counsel you to avoid: no, you must embrace them, and love them, and never be seen without them. Oh, how sovereign are these virtues, mistresses of all created things, empresses of the world, our deliverers from all the snares and entanglements laid by the devil, so dearly loved by our Teacher, Christ. Who was never for a moment without them! He that possesses them can safely go out and fight all the united forces of hell and the whole world and its temptations. Let him fear none, for his is the kingdom of the heavens. There is none whom he fear, for he cares nothing if he loses everything, nor does he count this as loss: his sole fear is that he may displease his God and he begs him to nourish these virtues within him lest he lose them through any fault of his own.[17]

In this passage, St. Teresa speaks to us of how detachment has a close kinship with the virtue of humility. Thus, as we detach ourselves from material things and endeavor to perform loving works of charity, we need to be humble in our approach. We do not want to appear to others to take pride in our actions or to seem judgmental of anyone else.

As an example, I am introvert, and I have a propensity towards what I call "extreme empathy." I always want to make other people feel comfortable, and, therefore, take on their anxiety and concerns in such a way that I hope makes them feel better. I literally sweat for people when they are giving presentations or otherwise engaging in public speaking engagements that make the majority of the population nervous! My intent is to lessen myself so that that person can feel built up, but do I always implement that intent perfectly? Indeed not, and this is merely one way in which I need to be vigilant about my own humility.

I love St. Teresa's words here about how these virtues benefit our souls: "He that possesses them can safely go out and fight all the united forces of hell and the whole world and its temptations. Let him fear none." This is a very mighty image that she presents us with! Our humility and detachment are quite powerful in the face of our enemy. The only thing we should fear is displeasing God. If we focus on that, our goal of walking in holiness has a much greater chance of success.

As I say, it is most important—all-important, indeed—that they should begin well by making an earnest and most determined resolve not to halt until they reach their goal, whatever may come, whatever may happen to them, however hard they may have to labour, whoever may complain of them, whether they reach their goal or die on the road or have no heart to confront the trials which they meet, whether the very world dissolves before them. Yet again and again people will say to us: "it is dangerous," "So-and-so was lost through doing this," "Someone else got into wrong ways," "Some other person, who was always praying, fell just the same," "It is bad for virtue," "It is not meant for women, it may lead them into delusions," "They would do better to stick to their spinning," "These subtleties are of no use to them," "It is quite enough for them to say their Paternoster and Ave Maria." With this last remark, sisters, I quite agree. Of course it is enough! It is always a great thing to base your prayer on prayers which were uttered by the very lips of the Lord[18]

This particular quote is loaded with information and subtleties, and shows us a lot about our St. Teresa! The topic that she is addressing throughout is prayer, and she starts off by discussing tenaciousness in our prayer life, saying they are "not to halt until they reach their goal...however hard they may have to labour, whoever may complain of them." For St. Teresa, there is no giving up when it comes to daily prayer. Spiritual dryness, busy schedules, others calling our attention in a different direction? Of course, we all experience those things. Regardless, we must persist in prayer. We cannot give up on this good fight! There is simply too much at stake.

St. Teresa, then, moves into a litany of reasons others have provided in criticism of prayer, or in criticism of the way someone else prayed. It sounds as if she has actually heard these things said to her because they are so specific: "They would do better to stick to their spinning." As a knitter who admires yarn on a daily basis, this one really captured my attention! St. Teresa lived in a much different time than you and I do with regards to treatment of women, yet it still is somewhat shocking to me that someone would say this. St. Teresa does not criticize this person, but her next comment speaks volumes: "'It is quite enough for them to say their Paternoster and Ave Maria.' With this last remark, sisters, I quite agree. Of course it is enough!" She is telling her sisters that they need not pay attention to the naysayers. They simply need to pray. Whether that prayer be in the form of traditional, scriptural prayers or in some other way, the important thing is to pray.

Let us now return to our vocal prayer, so that we may learn to pray in such a way that, without our understanding how, God may give us everything at once: if we do this, as I have said, we shall pray as we ought. As you know, the first things must be examination of conscience, confession of sin and the signing of yourself with the Cross. Then, daughter, as you are alone, you must look for a companion—and who could be a better Companion than the very Master Who taught you the prayer that you are about to say? Imagine that this Lord himself is at your side and see how lovingly and how humbly he is teaching you— and, believe me, you should stay with so good a Friend for as long as you can before you leave him. If you become accustomed to having him at your side, and if he sees that you love him to be there and are always trying to please him, you will never be able, as we put it, to send him away, nor will he ever fail you. He will help you in all your trials and you will have him everywhere. Do you think it is a small thing to have such a Friend as that beside you?[19]

I love St. Teresa's instructions for us on prayer. First, she sets up an ideal way for us to start our daily prayer. We should examine our consciences, confess any sins that we may have committed, and make the Sign of the Cross. In the previous passage, she had spoken to us about perseverance in prayer, and this moves nicely into a practical way for us to structure our daily time with the Lord. Personally, I tend to only examine my conscience prior to going to confession, and this is a very bad habit! St. Teresa is including this as a daily part of our routine, and this is a challenge that I need to take up.

Then, she speaks to us about our gaze when we are praying. St. Teresa tells us that we should envision the Lord right beside us while we pray. He is our best friend, and he is the author of our prayer. He is, indeed, the perfect companion for us! I love this characterization of the Lord as our friend and companion. He is our Father, yes, but he serves in many roles for us. "He will help you in all your trials and you will have him everywhere." Is there anything more soothing than this thought? As we go about our daily lives, our jobs, and our other responsibilities, the Lord is right there with us, everywhere.

"Our Father, which art in the heavens." O my Lord, how Thou dost reveal Thyself as the Father of such a Son, which Thy son reveals himself as the Son of such a Father! Blessed be Thou for ever and ever. Ought not so great a favour as this, Lord to have come at the end of the prayer? Here, at the very beginning, Thou dost fill our hands and grant us so great a favour that it would be a very great blessing if our understanding could be filled with it so that the will would be occupied and we should be unable to say another word. Oh, how appropriate, daughters, would perfect contemplation be here! Oh, how right would the soul be to enter within itself, so as to be the better able to rise above itself, that this holy Son might show it the nature of the place where he says His Father dwells—namely, the heavens! Let us leave earth, my daughters, for it is not right that a favour like this should be prized so little, and that, after we have realized how great this favour is, we should remain on earth any more.[20]

I once read an article in which the author advocated going through the words of the Our Father prayer very slowly, meditating upon each word. I recall him commenting on the fact that we could take the first two words of this prayer, "our Father," which come directly from Scripture, and spend a lifetime contemplating just these. When I read these verses, this is the very first thought that jumped into my mind: St. Teresa, too, could spend an eternity dwelling on God as her Father.

This can be a deeply complex issue for many women, depending upon her relationship with her earthly father. I am very lucky in that I have a wonderful father, who has always been a blessing to me, and I hope to savor time on earth with him for many years to come. It is not like this for everyone, and for those lacking an earthly father figure, contemplating God as Father may be a painful issue. What I am gleaning from St. Teresa is that having God as our ultimate Father is a special blessing that we may not fully grasp the magnitude of until we reach heaven. Thus, whatever the nature of our identity as daughter, what we should focus on is that God loves us very much, and that it is all right if we do not fully understand the Fatherly relationship with him here on earth. This is a tremendous gift, that we have God as Father, and to try our best to contemplate it and God's love for us is enough for now.

O Eternal Wisdom! O good Teacher! What a wonderful thing it is, daughters, to have a wise and prudent Master who foresees our perils! This is the greatest blessing that the spiritual soul still on earth can desire, because it brings complete security. No words could ever exaggerate the importance of this. The Lord, then, saw it was necessary to awaken such souls and to remind them that they have enemies, and how much greater danger they are in if they are unprepared, and since if they fall it will be from a greater height, how much more help they need from the Eternal Father. So, lest they should fail to realize their danger and suffer deception, he offers these petitions so necessary to us all while we live in this exile: "And lead us not, Lord, into temptation, but deliver us from evil."[21]

Here we come to the end of the Our Father. St. Teresa is speaking to us today about temptation—how it is a reality for us and how we should deal with it. The fact that our Father foresees our perils brings me comfort! They will come, and when they do, we must be prepared. St. Teresa points out here that in seeking God, as we are all doing, we put ourselves in a greater position of injury should we fall victim to the temptations we are faced with. We are human, and so however important it is for us to realize our vulnerability to our enemy, we will, at least at times, fail to do this. This is where the last line of the Our Father is something we should pray with conviction regularly: "And lead us not, Lord, into temptation, but deliver us from evil." When we do fail (and we will), we pray for the Lord to deliver us from the resulting chaos. First and foremost, we need to pray that we will not fall into temptation. When that does occur, though, we put our faith and trust in the Lord that he can deliver us.

Conclusion

Our time with St. Teresa was a bit different from the other holy men and women whom we have studied, though still incredibly fruitful! St. Teresa's religious life was spent with her sisters, and that is where her focus lay with regard to holiness and spirituality. Nevertheless, as secular women, we, too, are called to holiness within our state in life, and we can draw a lot of wisdom from St. Teresa's writings.

First, St. Teresa speaks to us of detachment from material things. She was adamant that her Carmelite sisters focus solely on the spiritual realm and on Christ's love for them and their vocation. Our lives are different from theirs, certainly, but ultimately, all of us are dependent upon material goods for our shelter, food, clothing, and other necessities. That being the case, although we use and enjoy those things, our hearts should lie foremost with the Lord. Even in our jobs and responsibilities both inside and outside of the home, we should not let our focus linger on our material possessions. We can keep our gaze fixed on God and our heavenly reward.

Within that same theme, St. Teresa counsels us on humility. If we are humble, we will not feel the need to overwhelm our lives with material objects. As well, when we detach our hearts from material possessions, we need to be careful not to take pride in our actions. We do not want to give others a negative impression of our motives. When we turn our focus to the good of our souls, and to the souls of others, our motives must be pure. We should pray that a prideful perspective not take hold in our heart.

We also learn quite a bit about prayer from St. Teresa. She advises us that we must persevere in our prayer, and not take notice of the negativity of others whom we believe may not be doing it correctly. The important thing is to pray! We can converse with God in the silence of our hearts, or we can turn to familiar, traditional prayers from the Scriptures. St. Teresa tells us to set up daily prayer as a goal and not to let anything deter us from that. The ultimate goal is simply too important to let it fade away! Our enemy wishes to tempt us away from our life with Christ, and to successfully battle against these temptations, we must properly arm ourselves with prayer.

Finally, St. Teresa encourages us to spend time meditating on the Our Father, one of the first prayers we learned as children. Harkening back to St. Thérèse of Lisieux, we should assume a childlike wonder in God as our Father and in the words of the prayer his Son taught us. We could spend a lifetime meditating upon these words, and we should! God loves us and will always be there with us. We should envision him there with us as we pray.

We may not be cloistered Carmelite sisters like St. Teresa and her community, but we are all called to perfection and holiness within the vocation that God gave us. We can all aspire to the close union with God that St. Teresa shows us.

An Invitation to Ponder

Am I persevering in my daily prayer? What types of distractions often steal my prayer time, and what are two things I can do to eliminate those distractions? In what ways can I pray without ceasing during my daily routine?

_____

_____

_____

_____

_____

_____

_____

_____

_____

_____

_____

Connecting to Scripture

PRAYER TO THE HOLY SPIRIT BEFORE READING SCRIPTURE

Come, Holy Spirit. Guide me in receiving the message, lovingly personalized just for me, awaiting me here in God's Word. Open my *heart to understand and accept what the Scriptures can teach me today. Amen.*

☞ Proverbs 15:33 _____

_____

_____

☞ Luke 4:1–14 _____

_____

_____

☞ John 12:25–26 _____

_____

_____

☞ Colossians 4:2–6 _____

_____

_____

☞ 1 Thessalonians 5:17–22 _____

_____

_____

9 1 John 3:1–3 _____

_____

_____

Scripture Reflection

St. Teresa speaks frequently of detachment, and John 12:25 fits perfectly with our striving for detachment of self: "Whoever loves his life loses it, and whoever hates his life in this world will preserve it for eternal life." I do not believe that by this Jesus meant that he wants us to be miserable and unhappy in our earthly lives. He simply wants us to examine our hearts and look at our intentions. Being happy and content is a good thing, and, of course, our friends and family often bring us that happiness. In the end, though, God is our Creator. Without him, we would have nothing—no material possessions, no emotional happiness. We need to recognize that all of our hope and joy originates in him. When we recognize that, we keep our hearts and minds in proper focus to make good choices, to live lovingly and charitably, and to stay on a course for eternal life in heaven.

Our fear of the Lord is a crucial part of our spiritual walk, but the use of the word "fear" should not make our hearts feel apprehensive, which is how I felt about this phrase as a child. Proverbs 15:33 instructs us that "the fear of the Lord is training for wisdom," and, thus, our fear of our Father represents respect, a watchful eye on his instructions. In the face of this, when we are humble, this represents a crowning achievement above any earthly honor. We need to be humble before him and before our friends and family here on earth as well.

In our humility, we are to persevere in prayer and let our speech always be gracious, "seasoned with salt," as we are instructed in Colossians 4:2–6, so that we will know how we should respond to each other. St. Paul could be talking about a few things here, but most likely he means that we should season our speech with wisdom and stronger words when necessary. Indeed, this is precisely what St. Teresa would have us do. We should pray, always, regardless of what anyone says to us about it.

When we envision the Lord with us throughout the day, as our companion along for the ride, it is much easier to imagine the ability to pray without ceasing, as we are directed to do in 1 Thessalonians 5:17. When I was younger, I imagined the only people capable of prayer without ceasing to be cloistered nuns and monks. Now I know that the situation is much more complex than that. We may not be able to sit in silent prayer for any length of time during our days, but we can still pray. We can offer up our actions for that particular day, we can turn our minds to God in the few quiet moments we do have, and we can invite Jesus into our tasks before we complete them, even if distraction and noise reign from then on.

God wants to minister to us as his children, even though we may see him much differently than when we were young children. Since I became an adult and had my own little ones, I do not often think of myself in a child's role anymore. To my parents, however, I am still very much their little girl. They want to help me and guide me just as much as they always did, albeit in a different way. To God, we are always his children, regardless of our age. He always loves us and wants what is best for us. He wants to guide us, but we do have free will. I struggle with this at times because I want to control things so that they do not turn out in a way that I see as bad or hurtful. Our control, though, is quite limited, whether or not we accept this. From 1 John 3:2, "What we shall be has not yet been revealed." God is our Father, and he knows what we shall be, what choices we are going to make. We do not need to worry about what is to come. We need to keep our eyes focused on him, and he can take care of the rest.

Inevitably, we will be faced with situations of temptation. Jesus, being both fully God and fully human, was also susceptible to temptation during his earthly life. We see in the Gospel of Luke 4:1–14 that Jesus was able to ward off the different temptations that Satan puts before him. The difference is that Jesus was full of the Holy Spirit. He had also prepared himself by fasting and praying for forty days leading up to those temptations. How often do we fall into temptation because we are not setting ourselves up spiritually for success? For example, how often do we neglect our prayer life or neglect small opportunities to sacrifice and hone our focus on the Lord? We can better organize ourselves for resisting temptations by preparing our souls on a regular basis through daily prayer and regular reception of the sacraments. We can succeed if we take the appropriate steps.

An Invitation to Share

1. In what ways was the group still able to relate to St. Teresa of Avila given the difference in time period and intended audience?

_____

_____

_____

_____

_____

_____

_____

_____

_____

_____

_____

_____

_____

_____

_____

_____

2. As twenty-first-century women, in what specific ways can we become detached from our material possessions and more focused on Christ?

_____

_____

_____

_____

_____

_____

_____

_____

_____

_____

_____

3. How do our prayer lives differ from that of St. Teresa, who lived in a cloistered religious community? How can St. Teresa's wisdom bolster our prayer lives?

_____

_____

_____

_____

_____

_____

_____

_____

_____

4. In what ways can we create a domestic monastery for ourselves in our prayer lives and in our homes?

_____

_____

_____

_____

_____

_____

_____

_____

_____

Closing Prayer

Dear Lord, thank you for bringing us together to study your Word and the teachings of the great St. Teresa of Avila. We pray, Lord, that St. Teresa intercede for us to live good and holy lives, from among her place in the great cloud of witnesses in heaven. We pray for her perseverance in prayer and for her ability to eschew the worldly gains this life has to offer, in favor of a closer relationship with Our Lord.

We long to be with you, Lord, and we covet your companionship in our prayers. Help us to be up to the task of praying without ceasing and to humbly do your will throughout our lives. We ask this in the precious name of Jesus. Amen.

4: Introduction to the Devout Life

Opening Prayer

Dear Lord, guide us as we read the wisdom of St. Francis de Sales. He has so much to teach us about everyday holiness and about how we can achieve such holiness amid our family lives and careers. Help me, Lord, to have the faith of St. Francis de Sales that close union with you is within reach for me every single day.

I long for the encouragement to frequent the sacraments and for the vibrant, ongoing life of prayer that St. Francis de Sales displayed. Help me to strive for this, Lord, and to achieve it. In the spiritual warfare that is our earthly existence, I want to stay close to your side, dear Lord.

Guide us, Lord, in not letting the anxieties of this world crush our spirits nor divert our focus from you. Help us to emulate Mary, when our emotions would have us be Martha. We ask this in the precious name of Jesus.

Amen.

On My Heart

_____

_____

_____

_____

_____

_____

_____

_____

_____

_____

_____

_____

_____

The Blessing of St. Francis de Sales

Confession: I have had a saint crush on St. Francis de Sales for quite a few years now. In fact, my copy of _Introduction to the Devout Life_ is dog-eared and highlighted from when I read it back in my twenties, and it's been nearly two decades since then! I was drawn to this book and this saint all those years ago because at the time, I was craving guidance in my spiritual life, as well as deeper union with God. Someone recommended _Introduction to the Devout Life_ to me, and I was immediately struck by how useful and practical the text was, without being a heavy and difficult read.

St. Francis de Sales was a priest who lived in the seventeenth century. Despite those two things that strongly distinguish him from our situation as twenty-first-century laywomen, St. Francis writes in a very relatable style and focuses on the needs of those living in the world. Many of the classical works of Church literature written in St. Francis' time were directed at religious men and women who had withdrawn from the world, as we saw in the last chapter with St. Teresa of Avila. St. Francis, on the other hand, was a missionary who wanted to minister to Calvinists who had left the Catholic faith. He wanted his writings to inspire and encourage everyday people of faith, with families and secular jobs. I found St. Francis' writings meaningful twenty years ago, and I find them just as much so now. I hope that you find as much fodder in his teachings to apply to your daily faith walk as I do!

Reflection on Selections from *Introduction to the Devout Life*

The work of purging the soul cannot and should not end except when our life itself ends. We must not be disturbed by our imperfections, since for us perfection consists in fighting against them. We cannot fight them unless we see them, or overcome them unless we face them. Our victory does not consist in being unconscious of them but in not consenting to them. Not to consent to them is to be displeased with them. To practice humility is absolutely necessary for us to suffer wounds at times in this spiritual warfare, but we are never vanquished unless we lose our life or our courage. Imperfections and venial sins cannot deprive us of spiritual life; it is lost only by mortal sin. It only remains for us, therefore, not to lose courage...Fortunate for us, we are always victorious in this war, as long as we are willing to fight.[22]

Reading this verse, my first thought is that St. Francis de Sales may have been an inspiration for some of Pope St. John Paul II's works! Modern day spiritual warfare and courage in the face of these every-day struggles, was a big theme for St. John Paul II. St. Francis uses words like "fight," "victory," and "overcome," and this lends a bit more excitement to the daily struggle against sin, at least in my mind.

As St. Francis reminds us, our work to overcome daily temptations towards sin, our constant rise and fall between sinning and picking ourselves up to try again—this is a constant cycle throughout our earthly lives. We should not allow ourselves to sink into despair because we recognize our own weaknesses and see the things that we normally fall prey to. It is actually a *good* thing to be aware of these items because it means we can be more fully armed to battle them. It is not awareness that is the problem in this scenario; it is our consent to them. If we withhold consent to the sin, then we are getting somewhere in our battle against evil.

As I reflect on these words, my mind immediately goes to an epic battle scene between good and evil forces, as portrayed in some high budget Hollywood film. This is likely not what St. Francis had in mind, but I think it is apt all the same! The battle for our souls is no small matter. We should keep it in its proper place within our focus and act accordingly. We are victorious as long as we are willing to fight.

If we are truly humble, our sins will be infinitely offensive to us since God is offended by them. When you kneel before your confessor, imagine that you are on Mt. Calvary at the feet of Jesus crucified and remember that it is the merits of his Precious Blood which now cleanses you. Declare every-thing with candor and simplicity so that your conscience may be completely at rest. This done, listen to the priest's advice and direction and say within your heart, 'Speak, Lord, for your servant is listening.'[23]

I love the practical imagery St. Francis presents us with here. My impression is that, like me, many people struggle with going to the sacrament of Reconciliation. I put off going as long as possible because I find it uncomfortable to be in the confessional, telling another person about the sins that I have committed of my own free will. St. Francis tells us to imagine that we are right up on Mt. Calvary with Jesus, at his feet and looking up at him crucified. With that powerful image in our minds, we must remember that it is because of this sacrifice that we are about to be forgiven for the sins that we have committed.

Then we come to the tough part: opening our mouths to vocalize the sins we have undertaken. St. Francis advises us to be simple and candid about this difficult task. The only place to start is at the beginning, yes? Start there, and unburden your heart. In this way, our consciences will have no lingering doubts or feelings of guilt. After that, our only other course of action is to listen to the priest's advice, undertake our penance, and ask the Lord to speak to us in the silence of our hearts. We are now open to fully listen to him.

After finishing your mental prayer, watch against disturbing the inner peace it bestows. If possible, keep silence for a while and quietly transfer your heart from prayer to other duties. Should you meet someone on the way home, or even at the church door, with whom you must converse, do so, of course, but still try to preserve your tranquility. You must learn how to go from prayer to duties brought on by your vocation and state of life. The lawyer must be able to pass from prayer to pleading cases, the merchant to commerce, the housewife to the care of her household, and so forth. Since both prayer and the duties of your state in life are both in conformity with God's will, you must pass from one to the other with a devout and quiet mind.[24]

Can you see now why I love St. Francis de Sales so much? He understand us, yes?! What he is describing above, I struggle with every single day. I wake up in the morning, get my kids off to school, have a lovely breakfast and cup of coffee with my husband, pray my rosary in the car, and then I arrive at work. This is inevitably when my calm and collected mental state begins to deteriorate. When I get into my office, a red voicemail indicator light and dozens of emails demand my attention, and I notice myself feeling frazzled. By the time I head off to teach my first class of the day, my mood is much more on edge, and I am more prone to becoming irritated than I was several hours earlier.

This is exactly what St. Francis is speaking of in this selection. Always, we should try to preserve our inner tranquility. This is not to say that it is easy, but when we have the Lord in our life, and when we know that our vocation and state in life is his will for us, what is there to be frazzled about? Of course, it is our human nature for that to happen, but if we shift our focus a bit, we may be able to battle against this. Of course, St. Francis is right there to intercede for us in our spiritual battles!

We should tend to our worldly concerns with care and diligence, but not with solicitude, worry or anxiety. The angels have care for our salvation and they do it diligently, but not with anxiety. Care and diligence may be accompanied with tranquility and peace of mind, but they are weakened by worry and solicitude and certainly by anxiety. Be attentive, of course, to all the matters God commits to your care. Since God has confided them to you, he wishes you to take good care of them. Don't exert yourself over them with undue forwardness or uneasiness. Don't worry about them because worry clouds reason and good judgment and prevents us from doing a good job with the very things that cause the worries. [25]

When I read this verse, I feel like St. Francis has come down from heaven, right in front of my face, just to have a conversation with me. I am a worrier. I have been since I was a child. I was that anxious kid in school, always worried that I was going to get in trouble for something, or that I had not done an assignment correctly. As an adult, that anxiety has transferred to worries for the health and safety of my own children, and generally to situations that arise at work and in my personal life. St. Francis is, of course, absolutely correct that worry clouds our ability to reason, and, thus, we should not let it take root, lest it prevent us from doing a good job, which is what we are actually worried about anyway!

I love his example that the angels have been given a pretty important task—they are guiding us towards salvation, and, yet, they have no anxiety over it despite the enormity of the undertaking. We should take care in our responsibilities and do our best. That is what God is tasking us to do. Elevating that care to the level of anxiety is not only destructive to our inner peace, it is also counterproductive. If you are like me, you may struggle with this advice for a lifetime. Without recognizing this truth, however, our souls would be in a much weaker position.

Our Savior is pleased to accept the great deeds of devotion as well as the least and lowest deeds. To serve him as he wishes, we must take care to serve him well both in great, lofty matters and in small, unimportant things. With love we can capture his heart by the one just as well as by the other. Be ready to suffer many sacrifices for Our Lord, whether it is martyrdom or the loss of our loved ones. Prepare your heart for all such sacrifices. However, if Divine Providence does not demand such great things from you, prepare to offer what does come your way. Bear patiently the slight injuries, the little inconveniences, the inconsequential losses and the like that daily come your way. These little daily acts of charity, this headache, toothache, cold, bad humor from a loved one, this broken glass, this contempt or scorn, the loss of a glove, the little inconveniences incurred by going to bed early and getting up early to pray and go to Mass—in short, all such trivial trials when accepted and embraced with love are highly pleasing to God's mercy. These things may occur from moment to moment, so store up these to form a great treasure of spiritual riches.[26]

When I read this selection, St. Thérèse of Lisieux immediately comes to mind. She, too, spoke to us of using small sacrifices to offer up a spiritual bouquet of sorts for the greater glory of God. She called this her "little way of holiness," and it is what she is most known for. St. Francis predates our lovely St. Thérèse, so, perhaps, he was her inspiration for her own faith walk! I also like the very specific spin he puts on this technique for achieving holiness, making it very relatable for laypeople. His little daily acts of charity include enduring a headache, losing an item that is key to our comfort in our daily commute, getting out of bed earlier than you would like to, and tolerating "bad humor from a loved one." (I translate this to mean a moody spouse, or child who woke up on what I call the "sassy side of the bed.") St. Francis' mission was to reach out to those in a station of life very different from his own, and I love how he brings his spiritual advice to a level of absolute practicality and wit.

When we accept these small injuries throughout our day, even embrace them, we do something that is "highly pleasing to God's mercy." Of course, larger sacrifices may come into play as well. St. Francis mentions the death of loved ones and martyrdom as things that are obviously on a completely different level from the annoyances that crop up in daily life. We need to be prepared to deal with such tragedies and to have our hearts ready if God asks this of us. More frequently, though, he is going to ask us for these small sacrifices. When I see the things that creep up in my day as these lovely flowers I can offer to God for his own purposes, it certainly makes those stressful situations seem infinitely more meaningful and bearable!

Oppose any tendency to sadness and melancholy. Although it may seem as if everything you do is cold, sluggish and sad, you must persevere. By means of sorrow the Devil tries to make us weary of good works. If he sees that we do not stop our good works, but go on meritoriously persevering, he will cease his attacks. It is good to occupy ourselves in exterior works and to very them as much as possible. This diverts the soul from depressing subjects and purifies and warms our spirits, for sorrow is a passion in cold, dry dispositions.[27]

I strongly relate to this passage because I am a person who has suffered from depression in the past. In my case, it was of the postpartum variety, but, of course, depression affects many people in all different circumstances of life. Without minimizing that this is to a large extent outside of our control, St. Francis wants to encourage us in our struggle. Even when we struggle, we can persevere, and that is what St. Francis is advising us to do. He reminds us that it's the devil who tries to make it appear as if everything we do is without merit. Our perseverance will yield fruit.

He also reminds us that keeping our minds and hands busy will help to dissuade the sadness from pervading our lives. When I read this, I immediately thought of a genre of books I enjoy reading—Amish fiction. These are very sweet tales of relationships and romance that are set within Amish communities. One of the tenets of faith that comes up often in these books is that one should not remain idle for long, lest you grant entrance to the devil where you do not want him. I think that it is this same bit of wisdom that St. Francis is asking us to employ here. If we know that we are feeling down on a given day, try to keep busy. When our minds and hands are busy at work, we allow less space for the sadness to fester and potentially negative results to occur.

Conclusion

After spending some time with St. Francis de Sales, you are likely as enamored with him as I am. Despite being a priest and living in a very different time than we do, he is so wise and understanding of the roles laypeople play in the Church and in the everyday lives of other people. St. Francis shares a number of things with us that I endeavor to carry forward into a new semester of teaching, and these fit, of course, with whatever your job or responsibilities entail.

St. Francis encourages us to be courageous and to always take heart. As we journey through our days, we will encounter temptations. Sometimes, we will fall to these temptations. St. Francis, though, advises us that victory in these challenges lies simply in being aware that we are imperfect and in continuing to strive for holiness. Remaining in denial of our weaknesses and/or not trying to improve ourselves is where we could truly fail. Our efforts in this regard are what will strengthen us and what will please God.

Given our imperfect state, regular reception of the sacrament of Reconciliation is crucial. St. Francis suggests that we picture Jesus next to us as we kneel in the confessional and that we think of actually being on Mt. Calvary as we confess our sins. Connecting with our Savior in this way will aid us in fully cleansing our souls when we receive this sacrament, and that is key to remaining strong for the spiritual warfare we face each day.

Confession also has the benefit of creating a spirit of interior peace, another thing that St. Francis teaches as the crux of day-to-day holiness. Regardless of our state in life, following our prayer time with the Lord, we need to endeavor to carry forward that peace throughout our day. In this way, we will find more opportunities for charitable outreach to others and to be able to see more fully God's hand in our everyday interactions.

St. Francis also counsels us to do our best in battling our proclivity to anxiety and sadness. As we move about our day and situations arise that cause us anxiety, irritation, or defensiveness, we can offer up these things for God's glory. Nothing is too small to be useful in God's greater Kingdom.

St. Francis has given us a lot of practical advice for holiness in day-to-day living. Now it is up to us to implement it!

An Invitation to Ponder

With what sin do I struggle the most on a daily basis? Do I immediately turn to God when I see this temptation approaching? What things in my daily routine give rise to temptations to sin and to disrupt my inner peace? Are there ways I can eliminate these temptations or otherwise mitigate them?

_____

_____

_____

_____

_____

_____

_____

_____

_____

_____

_____

Connecting to Scripture

PRAYER TO THE HOLY SPIRIT BEFORE READING SCRIPTURE

Come, Holy Spirit. Guide me in receiving the message, lovingly personalized just for me, awaiting me here in God's Word. Open my heart to understand and accept what the Scriptures can teach me today. Amen.

❧ 1 Samuel 3:7–18 _____

_____

_____

❧ Psalm 54:6–9 _____

_____

_____

❧ Psalm 138 _____

_____

_____

❧ Luke 1:46–55 _____

_____

_____

⑦ Luke 10:38-41 _____

_____

_____

⑦ 1 Corinthians 10:31-33 _____

_____

_____

Scripture Reflection

As we go through our daily struggles with sin, God is at our side. Psalm 54:6 reminds us that "God is present as my helper." We need only remember to turn to him. He sustains us and is always there to help us. Thankfully, he is faithful to us. He will always be there to guide us and to assist us in vanquishing our foes, our sins, if we turn to him. As an introvert, I tend to want to fight battles on my own. I am afraid to ask for help, or I feel that I do not need help. This is, of course, a fallacy. I always need God, and so do you. We are in this battle called life together, and God will take our hand whenever we desire and ask for it.

As I reflect on the story of the Lord summoning Samuel, as relayed in 1 Samuel 7-18, I am recalling the verses we explored from St. Francis. St. Francis emphasized how we must be brave in our spiritual battle against sinful temptations. In contemplating the sacrament of Reconciliation, we realize the close kinship between our spiritual strength and this particular sacrament is obvious. In our selection from Samuel, we journey along with him in listening to what God is trying to tell him. For Samuel to understand the Lord's request, he had to become aware that the Lord was present and could call out to him in this way; "Here I am. You called me," he repeatedly says to Eli. My takeaway from this story is the importance of listening. It is only when Samuel is made aware that the Lord could speak to him in this way that he finally responds: "Speak, for your servant is listening." When we prepare ourselves for confession, when we are sitting in the confessional with the priest, and when we pray our penance afterward, are we truly listening for God's voice? His shepherd is guiding us as we experience this sacrament. There is no better time to listen for the Lord than this.

Experiencing the grace that comes from Confession, I think immediately of maintaining that inner peace. Praying Psalm 138, we are doing so by praising God with our hearts and lips. The Lord has triumphed over all for us, and for this we will praise him forever. Even "though I walk in the midst of dangers, you guard my life when my enemies rage. You stretch out your hand; you right hand saves me" (Psalm 138:7). When I leave the peace and quiet of my morning prayer and move into the cacophony that is my workplace, I always try to remind myself that the Lord is by my side. He is our King, and he is triumphant over all the enemies that try to get to us this day. In the little temptations to impatience and ingratitude that are a part of my work day, I can think of the Lord stretching out his hand to me. In that way, at least sometimes, I hope to resist giving in to these temptations.

Indeed, in terms of temptations, there is none greater for me than that of nervous anxiety. I love the story of Martha and Mary from Luke 10:38–41 for this very reason. As you can already tell from several anecdotes in this Bible study, I play the part of Martha quite well. I am perpetually annoyed with Mary for not helping me enough as I whirl around the room, trying to get things done that I deem important, as my anxiety level rises with each passing moment. Martha thinks that what she is doing is so much more valuable than what Mary is doing. Jesus, though, corrects her. Mary, by sitting with him, relaxing her mind while she enjoys his company and learns from him, is actually doing a better thing for their guest. I need to learn from this story and to call it to mind often, especially at holiday time!

"Whatever you do, do everything for the glory of God." St. Paul, in 1 Corinthians 10:31, was advising the churches of this standard for living, even long ago in the years just after Jesus lived on earth. Their stresses at that time in history were much more likely to be of the larger variety, as we discussed previously. I am certain, though, that new Christians at that time were also dealing with hurt from loved ones who did not understand their newfound faith, thoughtless actions and words tossed their way, as well as in-fighting and differences of interpretation, even among their Christian brethren. St. Paul wanted them to offer up even those things for God's greater work. He can use these things, and so why should we withhold this healing opportunity from him? When we lose a single mitten from a pair or encounter a sulky coworker, we can offer up these occurrences to God. I will try to remember this as I go about my teaching days at work. We are in this together.

Our Blessed Mother is our greatest ally in offering up to the Lord everything we do. The canticle of Mary in Luke 1:46–55 is a particular balm for my soul. When this took place, her situation was not easy. She was unmarried and expecting a child, a great and, most likely, perplexing request had been made of her by God, and now she has come to visit her cousin to assist her in late pregnancy. Her spirit must have felt burdened and uneasy. Still, her soul proclaims the greatness of the Lord, and her spirit rejoices in God, her Savior. Indeed, God had looked down on her and chosen her for something special, and Mary recognized that as a wondrous thing even in the midst of her challenging life situation. Although God has not chosen us for something quite as special as Mary, he still chooses us each day to do things for him and to give glory to his kingdom.

Even when we are feeling down, God is there, and he is good. He is choosing us for himself, and he loves us. His mercy extends forever, and he has always helped those who have called out to him. He is there for us; we just have to hold out our hands.

An Invitation to Share

1. Everyone in the group please share a daily temptation they feel comfortable discussing. What are specific ways that we can battle known temptations?

_____

_____

_____

_____

_____

_____

_____

_____

_____

_____

_____

2. What is a practical way to start our days with prayer as St. Francis suggests? In what ways can we carry the resulting sense of interior peace throughout an entire day?

_____

_____

_____

_____

_____

_____

_____

_____

_____

3. Anxiety is a very real concern for many people. What are some prayers we can say, and who are some additional saints we can call upon to aid us in our endeavor to be strong in courage and less anxious about our daily affairs?

_____

_____

_____

_____

_____

_____

_____

_____

_____

_____

_____

_____

_____

4. What are examples of small things from our daily routines that we can offer up to God? Does anyone have an example of when this led to a positive and/or unexpected result?

_____

_____

_____

_____

_____

_____

_____

_____

_____

_____

_____

Closing Prayer

Dear Lord, thank you for giving us St. Francis de Sales as a teacher, a timeless gift to the Church. His enduring ability to speak to the lives of laypeople is an incredible blessing. We pray that he continue to inspire us as we go forth, striving for holiness in our everyday lives.

Lord, we know that we will face temptations to sin as we work within the stations of life you have given to us. We ask for the intercession of St. Francis to aid us in recognizing these temptations and in fighting them. We pray for his courage as we go about the tasks and relationships you have entrusted to our care. Guide us in recognizing your will and your hand in our interactions with others. We want to give ourselves the best opportunity to succeed, dear Lord. Help us to be like Mary, sitting and learning from you rather than being anxious about things that do not matter as much or that are totally outside of our control. We ask this in the precious name of Jesus.

Amen.

5: Essays on Woman

Opening Prayer

Dear Lord, help us to learn from the great wisdom and heroism of St. Edith Stein. She has so much to teach us about the unique gifts of women and feminine spirituality. Guide us, Lord, in applying our gifts to the best of our abilities within our state in life, and in striving to always imitate your holy mother, Mary.

We want to always live out our days, dear Lord, practicing charity and kindness, with love and understanding. Help us to present ourselves in such a way that others see you reflected in our actions. Shepherd us, Lord, in demonstrating the courage and spiritual strength of St. Edith Stein.

Guide us, Lord, in always standing firm in our convictions and in living out our feminine identity in accordance with your will. We ask this in the precious name of Jesus.

Amen.

On My Heart

_____

_____

_____

_____

_____

_____

_____

_____

_____

_____

_____

_____

_____

The Blessing of St. Edith Stein

St. Edith Stein was born in the late nineteenth century and became a noted German philosopher, studying under Edmund Husserl (who was also the mentor of Martin Heidegger). She was born into a Jewish family but became a proclaimed atheist as a young adult. After reading the works of St. Teresa of Avila, she became a devoted Catholic and, ultimately, a Discalced Carmelite nun. Taking the religious name Sister Teresa Benedicta of the Cross, she lived as a Carmelite sister during the early years of World War II and was murdered at the Auschwitz concentration camp in 1942.

As a twentieth-century academic and martyr, St. Edith Stein has always struck me as a relatable, modern woman with a dramatic story. She was a prolific writer, and her thoughts on womanhood and spirituality are profound. She has a lot to offer us by way of living out our femininity and offering our lives to God amid the different vocations and paths a woman's life may take. She spoke a lot about the gifts women have to offer their jobs and families and about how feminine spirituality is distinct from that of masculine spirituality. When I picked up *Essays on Woman,* I was so excited to learn from her, and I hope you are too! I felt like I was taking one of her university courses and am incredibly grateful that her writing has lived on to keep her legacy alive in the Church.

Reflection on Selections from *Essays on Woman*

Only subjective delusion could deny that women are capable of practicing vocations other than that of spouse and mother. The experience of the last decades and, for that matter, the experience of all times has demonstrated this. One could say that in case of need, every normal and healthy woman is able to hold a position. And there is no profession which cannot be practiced by a woman. A self-sacrificing woman can accomplish astounding achievements when it is a question of replacing the breadwinner of fatherless children, of supporting abandoned children or aged parents. But, also, individual gifts and tendencies can lead to the most diversified activities. Indeed, no woman is only *woman;* like a man, each has her individual specialty and talent, and this talent gives her the capability of doing professional work, be it artistic, scientific, technical, etc. Essentially, the individual talent can enable her to embark on any discipline, even those remote from the usual feminine vocations.[28]

St. Edith devotes many of her writings to advocating for the importance of women's roles as wives and mothers. This vocation is a natural part of our God-given femininity, and, as such, it should be held in the highest esteem. For the time that she lived, however, I think it is remarkable that St. Edith also acknowledges that for some women, this may not be their reality, at least at a certain point in their lives. As well, some women who are wives and mothers may also hold additional professional positions for the good of their families. Women are imbued with talents and skills that are widely applicable, and, thus, they should discern God's will for how best to use those in their individual situations.

The emphasis that you see in the above passage is actually that of St. Edith: "...no woman is only *woman.*" Being a woman is a remarkable thing. We are equal in dignity to, but distinct from, men. God made us this way. That aspect of us, however, is not all there is to our souls, our very beings. We have other interests and abilities, and some of these may even overlap with those of our male counterparts. Recognizing this is crucial to giving women the respect and esteem they rightly deserve.

It is the vocation of every Christian, not only of a few elect, to belong to God in love's free surrender and to serve Him. Whether man or woman, whether consecrated or not, each one is called to the imitation of Christ. The further the individual continues on this path, the more Christlike he will become. Christ embodies the ideal of human perfection: in Him all bias and defects are removed, and the masculine and feminine virtues are united and their weaknesses redeemed; therefore, His true followers will be progressively exalted over their natural limitations. This is why we see in holy men a womanly tenderness and a truly maternal solicitude for the souls entrusted to them while in holy women there is manly boldness, proficiency and determination.[29]

In this selection. St. Edith harkens back to Thomas á Kempis and his wisdom on imitating Christ. And her insight into this matter brings such a lovely feminine touch to the analysis. We are all called, men and women alike, to serve God and to imitate his Son, Jesus. Jesus, of course, demonstrated all of the qualities a holy person should, and, in fact, those are both traditionally male *and* traditionally female qualities. I love how St. Edith makes this point—as women we are indeed much different from men. That being the case, our femininity is only enhanced by emulating the matter-of-fact courage and determination that we often see in men. Holy men only enhance their masculinity by embracing a tender, nurturing disposition toward those in their care.

We should always aim for virtue, and in Christ we see those all exemplified. As women, we are not trying to be like men. We are trying to bring to life all of the virtuous qualities that Christ embodied.

It is most important that the Holy Eucharist become life's focal point: that the Eucharistic Savior is the center of existence; that every day is received from His hand and laid back therein; that the day's happenings are deliberated with Him. In this way, God is given the best opportunity to be heard in the heart, to form the soul, and to make its faculties clear-sighted and alert for the supernatural. It then comes about of itself that one sees the problems of one's own life with God's eyes and that one learns to resolve them in His spirit. For this, a peaceful and clear-headed consideration of exterior facts and events must emerge. Whoever lives in the strong faith that nothing happens without the knowledge and will of God is not easily disconcerted by astonishing occurrences or upset by the hardest of blows. He will stay quiet and face the facts clearly; he will discover the right guidelines for his practical behavior in the overall situation.[30]

St. Edith is certainly speaking to my heart with this passage. I am a person who tends to retreat into her own head a lot and not necessarily to talk to our Lord! I am simply an introvert who always has a lot on her mind, and this is not the ideal way to live out our days. Each day, we need to give God the best opportunity to be heard in our lives. In this way, we will be better equipped to resolve problems in accordance with his will and generally discern God-driven decisions. A large part of the way that we can accomplish this is through receiving the Eucharist frequently and in keeping that as the focal point of our day. Too often, my own mind is awhirl with all of the tasks that I want to accomplish that day. I think that this is fairly normal, but I do not need to wallow in that place unnecessarily. Jesus has given us his Body to sustain us—our lives should be a testament to this! Instead of focusing on myself and what I wish to get done that day, I should focus on Jesus. I should focus on his sacrifice for us, but I should also focus on the way that he is present with us each day and is there for us whenever we pray to him.

I was also struck by St. Edith's words that for those who have a strong faith in the fact that nothing happens without God's knowledge and loving hand, they will not be so easily flustered, even by larger tragedies in life. This is difficult advice to implement, but I know that she is correct. It is not that God wants us to suffer. Our earthly lives, though, are going to contain some suffering—it is simply the nature of the world that we live in. God, however, will never abandon us. We need to firm up our faith in the truth that he is always present in our lives, just a prayer away.

Now begins the day's work, perhaps the teaching profession—four or five hours, one after the other. That means giving our concentration there. We cannot achieve in each hour what we want, perhaps in none. We must contend with our own fatigue, unforeseen interruptions, shortcomings of the children, diverse vexations, indignities, anxieties. Or perhaps this is office work: give and take with disagreeable supervisors and colleagues, unfulfilled demands, unjust reproaches, human meanness, perhaps also distress of the most distinct kind...each one must know, or get to know, where and how she can find peace. The best way, when it is possible, is to shed all cares again for a short time before the tabernacle. Whoever cannot do that, whoever also possibly requires bodily rest, should take a breathing space in her own room. And when no other rest whatever is attainable, when there is no place in which to retreat, if pressing duties prohibit a quiet hour, then at least she must for a moment seal off herself inwardly against all other things and take refuge in the Lord. He is indeed there and can give us in a single moment what we need.[31]

When I read this particular passage in *Essays on Woman,* I could not stop the smile from spreading across my face and remaining there for the rest of the day. I picture St. Edith up in heaven, enjoying my amusement. In fact, every time I read this passage, I feel like she is right in the room with us!

Let us examine our typical day, shall we? Now, all of us may have different day-to-day situations for our daily routine: some may be stay-at-home mothers; some may be mothers who also work inside or outside of the home; some may be single; some may be married without children or without any children still living at home. Yet whatever our God-given circumstances may be, we are all united in our womanhood, and in our striving for holiness. How many of us struggle with "fatigue, unforeseen interruptions ... diverse vexations, indignities, anxieties"? I am thinking that the answer to that question is *ALL* of us! Her descriptions of the trials that come from an office workplace make me giggle anew: "disagreeable supervisors and colleagues, unfulfilled demands, unjust reproaches, human meanness" It is not always funny in the moment, of course, but I believe that we can all strongly relate to these very things in our previous or current workplaces. What I take away from this passage is multifold: when we experience stressors in our daily lives, to the best of our ability, we should retreat for a quiet moment alone with the Lord. If we cannot physically retreat, then we can retreat within the solitude of our own head for a few moments to pray and to refresh ourselves mentally. He is always there for us and can give us what we need even within a single moment. Also, St. Edith understands precisely what we are going through. We should always ask for her intercession!

This is only a small indication how the day could take shape in order to make room for God's grace. Each individual will know best how this can be used in her particular circumstances. It could be further indicated how Sunday must be a great door through which celestial life can enter into everyday life, and strength for the work of the entire week, and how the great feasts, holidays, and the seasons of Lent, lived through in the spirit of the Church, permit the soul to mature the more from year to year to the eternal Sabbath rest. It will be an essential duty of each individual to consider how she must shape her plan for daily and yearly living, according to her bent and to her respective circumstances of life, in order to make ready the way for the Lord. The exterior allotment must be different for each one, and it must also adjust resiliently to the change of circumstances in the course of time…As to the means which are suitable for bringing about union with the eternal, keeping it alive or also enlivening it anew—such as contemplation, spiritual reading, participation in the liturgy, popular services, etc.—these are not fruitful for each person and at all times. For example, contemplation cannot be practiced by all and always in the same way.[32]

After journeying with St. Edith through a typical work day, whether it be inside or outside of the home, we now address the one day per week when we should rest. St. Edith mentions how for some people, even taking a silent moment out of their hectic work day in which to pray can be a physical impossibility. Those people may be limited to moments of quiet reflection only within the confines of their own thoughts, amidst the noise around them. Bearing that in mind, Sunday can be a day during which we physically and spiritually recharge for the entire week ahead. We can load up our armor with fuel, if you will, to last us through a traditional work week. Leisure time, Mass, prayer, and general quiet relaxation should all take place on our Sundays.

In addition to Sundays, St. Edith points out that holidays, feast days, and the liturgical seasons of Advent and Lent are also ideal times in which to recharge our spirits. These types of special days on the Church calendar allow us to grow over the long term, such that we can more productively gain refreshment on Sundays throughout the year. I look forward to Advent and Lent each year as a way to challenge myself to try new things in my spiritual walk so that I do not feel stagnation setting in, and, thus, this perspective really appeals to me. The things that we may choose to do on these days in order to recharge—going to Mass more frequently, spiritual reading, contemplation, etc.—will vary from person to person. Indeed, St. Edith points out that for some people, certain things that are spiritually very fruitful for some (e.g. praying the Liturgy of the Hours, attending daily Mass) not only may not be practical for others but also may not bear the same positive spiritual fruit. St. Edith is so wise in such everyday spirituality as it relates to laypeople. She recognizes that, especially for women, routines can vary widely, and, thus, it is only logical that a lifelong spiritual walk will also vary greatly from woman to woman.

That is why an intimate bond exists between Mary and ourselves. She loves us, she knows us, she exerts herself to bring each one of us into the closest possible relationship with the Lord—that which we are above all supposed to be. Of course, this is true for all humanity, but most particularly for women. The maternity and bridehood of the *Virgo-Mater* is continued, so to speak, in their maternity, natural and supernatural, and in their life as brides of Christ. And just as the heart sustains the other organs of woman's body and makes it possible for them to function, so we may genuinely believe there is just such a collaboration of Mary with every woman wherever that woman is fulfilling her vocation as woman; just so, there is a collaboration of Mary with us in all works of the Church. But just as grace cannot achieve its work in souls unless they open themselves to it in free decision, so also Mary cannot function fully as a mother if people do not entrust themselves to her...She herself can form in her own image those who belong to her.[33]

I have a huge soft spot in my heart for our Blessed Mother, and so I was drawn to include this particular selection for our study with St. Edith. I credit Mary with my reversion back to the Church as a young adult, and it is because I felt so drawn to her as a mother figure. I knew she would not be angry with me for the way that I had gone astray. Instead, she would welcome me back with open arms and proceed to help and guide me back onto the right path.

St. Edith delves into that notion here. Whatever our vocation may be—whether we be mothers ourselves or not, religious or laywomen, married or single, Mary is collaborating with each one of us to live out our vocation to the best of our abilities in accordance with God's will. St. Edith notes, importantly, that Mary can aid us only though our free-will decision to allow her to do so. "She can form in her own image those who belong to her." To me there is something so sweet about a sense of emotionally belonging to another person. We can belong to Mary if we choose, and in so doing, we can allow her to form us in her own perfectly feminine image. Our earthly lives are not going to resemble hers exactly, it goes without saying, but Mary bore a lot of things that we can relate to even now—mundane, everyday tasks related to being a wife and mother, great emotional suffering, and tremendous responsibility for the welfare of others. She bore it without complaint and without resentment. To have her mold us in her image would be a great honor. We simply have to invite her in.

Conclusion

I have enjoyed our time with St. Edith immensely, and I hope that you have as well. She is a saint who speaks to my heart as a woman and daughter of our Lord. She shares a number of practical points with us about living out a life of holiness, nuanced with a perfect emphasis on femininity. Let us take a look at the important points St. Edith leaves with us.

St. Edith talks a lot about the various roles women play in the earthly realm. God gave us the capability of bearing life and becoming wives and mothers, though not all women experience these things during their lifetimes. We have a unique gift in this, but God does not call all of us to it. Women can take part in any number of different professions and will be interested in countless hobbies and talents. Whatever our role is, we should relish it as it is given to us by our Creator. There is no end to the roles and activities that he may call us to.

As well, St. Edith notes how, as women, we should strive to imitate Christ. Jesus embodied the ideal qualities of virtue, and these are both traditionally masculine and feminine qualities. Although we should delight in our God-given femininity, we should also aim to employ the positive and strong personality traits we often see in men.

After her conversion, St. Edith made the Eucharist the center of her life and faith, and we should do the same. Even if we cannot get to Mass every single day, we can receive the Eucharist with reverence on Sundays and maintain a regular schedule of going to the sacrament of Reconciliation so that we are always disposed to receive Jesus' Body. We can carry that thought of Jesus truly present in the Eucharist with us throughout the week, and we can use that image whenever we take quiet moments out of our busy days to talk to the Lord. Whenever our days seem particularly noisy and hectic, that is when we most need Jesus within the silence of our hearts. It may not be easy to achieve silence on some days, but even if only within our own minds, we still can commune with the Lord.

Sunday as our day of rest and receiving the Eucharist, can be a single day that sustains us through the six days that follow. On that day, we should carve out as much time for quiet refreshment as possible, especially if our days during the week are filled with noise. Liturgical seasons like Lent, and other special holidays and feast days, are opportunities for long term spiritual growth that we can use to maximize our recharging on the Sabbath day.

Finally, Mary is, of course, our guide in the feminine spiritual life. She sets the perfect example of balancing work and spirituality, and the path to holiness. If we offer ourselves to her, she will help us and guide us, as our intercessor, in our needs and desires.

St. Edith brings an academic touch to the discussion of the spiritual life, but she does it in a way that is understandable even to those who have not studied philosophy the way that she did. I am so grateful that her teaching remains a treasured legacy of the Church!

An Invitation to Ponder

Do I take enough quiet time with the Lord on Sundays? What are some things I can do to increase my spiritual rest and recharging practices on Sundays? How can I improve the way that I make the Eucharist the focal point of my day? Can I add to my schedule a weekly Mass or a stop at adoration, or incorporate a set aside time for prayer, specifically concentrating on Jesus truly present in the Eucharist?

_____

_____

_____

_____

_____

_____

_____

_____

_____

_____

_____

_____

Connecting to Scripture

PRAYER TO THE HOLY SPIRIT BEFORE READING SCRIPTURE

Come, Holy Spirit. Guide me in receiving the message, lovingly personalized just for me, awaiting me here in God's Word. Open my heart to understand and accept what the Scriptures can teach me today. Amen.

Genesis 1:27–31 _____

_____

_____

✐ Psalm 11 _____

_____

_____

✐ John 6:30-40 _____

_____

_____

✐ John 19:25-27 _____

_____

_____

✐ 1 Corinthians 12:4-11 _____

_____

_____

✐ Philippians 4:4-9 _____

_____

_____

Scripture Reflection

I have to remind myself sometimes that God made me the way that I am. Indeed, "there are different kinds of spiritual gifts ... to each individual the manifestation of the Spirit is given for some benefit," as we see in 1 Corinthians 12:4–7. The fact that I am a nerdy, bookish sort of person, who would rather hide indoors than attend an outdoor party, well, that is part of the talents God gave me. I enjoy taking care of my home. I love books and enjoy recommending stories to other people based on the types of books that they appreciate. This all fits naturally into my state in life and my vocation of being a wife and mother and, also, a librarian. Our life journey may or may not turn out the way we always envisioned that it would. Mine certainly includes some differences from the original way I planned it out! Either way, we can rest assured that God made us the way that we are for a reason. He loves us and has given us gifts that are perfectly suited for us.

As we learn right from the beginning, in the first chapter of Genesis, God made us in his image, and we should call this to the forefront of our minds whenever we are feeling down about ourselves. God sees something of himself in us, and, thus, who are we to think that we are not good enough? He also made us male and female, different from each other, yet equal in dignity and complementary to the other. When God created mankind, he had a plan, and everything fits together perfectly in his plan.

I go through stretches in my life when I feel adrift. I certainly experienced that as a twenty-something, searching for my ultimate vocation (married life versus the religious life). I still experience it now in small ways. My children are constantly growing and changing, and I often question my ability to parent them properly and come up with solutions to the new challenges they face. My job is not as new and exciting to me as it once was, and sometimes in my avocation of writing, I experience dry spells. I will often ask myself, "What is it that God wants me to do?" I need to remember that God has a plan for me, as he does for you. He knew what he was doing when he created each one of us, and he found it to be good.

Throughout life, inevitably, we will encounter tragedy and suffering. I am a sensitive person, so small things that may not bother other people can cause great emotional distress to me. When we have Jesus, though, we have the bread in which "whoever comes to me will never hunger, and whoever believes in me will never thirst," as we learn in John 6:35. We have the ultimate recourse, Jesus. We are still going to mourn the losses in our life, and on some days, many things may upset us. But we have *Jesus*. His Body will always sustain us; we just have to make the time for him. I often find that the days that seem the busiest, the most difficult to squeeze yet another errand into, are the days that I most need that time to stop and pray or to stop at adoration. When I make that time for Jesus, my day suddenly seems a lot more manageable.

As we move about our days, we should have confidence in the presence of God and in his goodness, as we see prominently in Psalm 11:1–4: "In the Lord I take refuge" and "God's eyes keep careful watch." Even when we feel rushed and hectic, when everything seems to be working against us, the Lord is there to be our refuge. He is there in the silence of our hearts and minds, even when our environment is far from quiet.

Lately, when my day feels particularly rushed and stressful, I challenge myself to try to see God in the distracting and frustrating situations that inevitably arise. A student who acts out in difficult ways may just need a listening ear and a kind word. Sometimes their behavior is a cry for help and attention. If we can be that help to him or her, surprising results can occur. I could be the conduit to making his or her day better, and that fact alone stirs up a hope in my heart. If I can hang on to that hope, I consider my day a success! The Lord is there for us, especially during these hectic times.

Hectic times should remind us that our joy and peace must always rest in the Lord, as St. Paul stresses in Philippians 4:4–9. We should "have no anxiety at all, but in everything, by prayer and petition, with thanksgiving, make your requests known to God." We can rest assured that he hears us. He may not answer us in the way that we expect, but he will always answer us. Once we have asked, we can allow peace to fill our minds and souls. We have a Father who loves us and will always take care of us. It is sometimes difficult to rest easy in this knowledge, of course. In our human nature, we still want to control the outcome that we believe will bring us less pain. Instead, we should be alert for the Lord's greater plan for our lives.

As we rest on Sundays, we should think about this peace entering into our hearts. Prayer may take different forms for all of us, but whatever way is most fruitful for you, engage in that on Sunday. That peace which "surpasses all understanding" can then enter our hearts and buoy our spirits for the rest of the week.

Throughout everything, Mary is our mother. It is such a simple concept, yet so vast at the same time. Jesus intended for her to be our mother, and he reminded us of this from the cross as the Gospel of John relays in 19:25–27. If we bring her into our heart, she will be our intercessor and never let us down. Chosen as she was to be the Mother of God's Son, how can we not marvel at her role in each of our lives? She raised Jesus, cared for him, and provided for his emotional needs as he grew. Having her to also pray for us and guide us on our own spiritual path is overwhelming, to say the least. This is an opportunity that we should not pass up!

An Invitation to Share

1. What are the virtuous qualities that Jesus exemplified, which men and women alike can seek to emulate?

_____

_____

_____

_____

_____

_____

_____

2. What are different ways in which a person can seek out quiet solitude with the Lord, even in the midst of a noisy, chaotic work day?

_____

_____

_____

_____

_____

_____

_____

_____

3. During an upcoming Liturgical season (either Advent/Christmas or Lent/Easter), or on an upcoming feast day, what are ways members of the group could recharge their spiritual walks?

Hello mi name is Maria

What does it mean to "offer yourself to Mary"? How has our Blessed Mother worked in the lives of the women in the group?

Closing Prayer

Dear Lord, thank you for calling us together to study your Word and the work of St. Edith Stein. We are so grateful that we can learn from St. Edith's incredible wisdom, courage, and witness all of these years after her death.

Lord, help us to imitate the brave example of St. Edith. Her courageous actions as well as her studied research and writing are an inspiration to us all. We pray that we live out our vocations and professions with the same holy determination as St. Edith, and that she will intercede for us as we journey through our earthly lives. Grant us, Lord, the strength and understanding to apply the lessons of St. Edith in our lives. We ask this in the precious name of Jesus.

Amen.

6: Crossing the Threshold of Hope

THE CATHOLIC CLASSICS

Opening Payer

Dear Lord, guide us in learning from the great example of unwavering faith shown to us by St. John Paul II, who possessed the ideal combination of a childhood faith that transformed into a deep, abiding, and studied faith as an adult. Help us to imitate his example, Lord, as we move through the challenging times in which we live. Help us to never falter in walking toward you on our earthly journey and to always remember St. John Paul II's words to "Be not afraid." We pray for the gift of St. John Paul II's courage, dear Lord.

Mary, our mother, St. John Paul II loved you and knew that you would lead him, and us, to your Son. Please intercede for us in our different feminine roles, vocations, and professions, that we will always set a positive example, as St. John Paul II did, and give glory to the Lord. Help us to live out the new evangelization with our lives and to never be afraid to be fishers of men when the Lord calls us. We ask this in the precious name of Jesus.

Amen.

On My Heart

_____

_____

_____

_____

_____

_____

_____

_____

_____

_____

_____

_____

_____

The Blessing of St. John Paul II

This Scripture study on the spiritual classics obviously includes many of my favorite saints. I have mentioned that previously, especially with regards to St. Francis de Sales, St. Thérèse of Lisieux, and St. Edith Stein. No one in the communion of saints though, aside from our Blessed Mother herself, commands my heart more that St. John Paul II. He is the pope of my childhood and young adulthood, the only pope I knew until I was thirty years old, newly married, and expecting my first child. When I faltered in my faith in my early twenties and stopped attending Mass, it was his rock-solid faith example, his pointing to Mary as our mother and intercessor, and his beseeching to "Be not afraid" that led me back to the Church. When he passed away in 2005, I cried and mourned him as if someone in my family had died. It is one of the great regrets of my life that I never met him in person.

The first non-Italian pope in over four hundred years, Karol Wojtyla changed the Church in the late twentieth century. His childhood experiences of losing his parents and brother, of growing up under the Nazi occupation of Poland, and of studying for the priesthood in the underground seminary all served to carve out his steadfast faith and courage in the face of the monumental task of leading the Church during a crucial time in history. *Crossing the Threshold of Hope* is the compilation of a set of questions on an array of faith-related topics, composed by a journalist in the late 1990's, and the written answers of John Paul II. The content ranges from the existence of God to the reality of evil in the world to how we can become involved in the new evangelization. St. John Paul II's faith and tireless passion for the Church continue to be a great source of inspiration for me, and this book reinforced that in abundance. I hope that you enjoy this time with the intimate thoughts of the great St. John Paul II as much as I did.

Reflection on Selections from *Crossing the Threshold of Hope*

With all of this, however, in face of the modern world's development, *there is an ever-increasing number of people who ask themselves or who feel more keenly the most essential questions: What is man?* What is the meaning of suffering, of evil, of death, which persist despite all progress? What are these victories, purchased at so high a cost, really worth? What can man offer to society and what can he expect from it? What will there be after this life? The Church believes that Christ, who died and was resurrected for the sake of all, continuously gives to man through His Spirit the light and the strength to respond to his higher destiny. Nor is there any other name under heaven given to the human race by which we are to be saved. The Church also believes *that the key, the center, and the purpose of all of human history, is found in its Lord and Master.*[34]

St. John Paul II was a philosopher, and so his focus on these deep questions is not surprising. He is right, as well, that even people with no lingering curiosity in philosophy as an academic discipline ponder questions such as: "Why do good people suffer?" and "What happens after we die?" These are questions most people struggle with at one point in their lives or another. For St. John Paul II, who risked his life in order to serve the Church, the answer is simple: we should look to the Church, and the Church points to Christ.

Our feelings on such big questions are rarely uncomplicated, so this answer may seem pat. In the end, though, Christ is truly a complex solution. When he was on earth as a man, he challenged people and social norms, and shook up the communities he visited. He changed the lives of people who followed him. He died a very public, humiliating, and painful death, and then rose from the dead. Now, from heaven, he sends us his Spirit to guide us on our path to him. His Spirit also guides the Church and its shepherds, who aid us in our journey. None of this is easy, but Christ has shown us that he understands, that he faced the issues we face and is there now to hold our hands while we do the same. We can receive his Body each day to sustain us as we go about all of this, and know that even when things seem very, very bad, he will never abandon us.

God is always on the side of the suffering. His omnipotence is manifested precisely in the fact that He freely accepted suffering. He could have chosen not to do so. He could have chosen to demonstrate His omnipotence even at the moment of the Crucifixion. In fact, it was proposed to Him: 'Let the Messiah, the King of Israel, come down now from the cross that we may see and believe.' (MK 15:34). But He did not accept that challenge. The fact that He stayed on the Cross until the end, the fact that on the Cross He could say, as do all who suffer: 'My God, my God, why have you forsaken me?' (Mk 15:34), has remained in human history *the strongest argument.* If the agony on the Cross had not happened, the truth that God is Love would have been unfounded.[35]

This passage follows perfectly from the previous selection's focus on Christ and his Church as the answer to our deeper questions on the meaning of life and death. Inevitably, we think of God the most when suffering comes our way, and this applies to people who also pray and seek God during other times in their lives, as well as to those who do not. Suffering, indeed, unites all of us regardless of where we are on our faith walk. Christ suffered when he lived on earth. He knew how important that was for us, for our salvation, and for our uniting to him in his example. We can know for certain how much he loves us because he suffered for us in this way.

St. John Paul II also suffered during his earthly life and related this to the sufferings of Christ. He lost his mother as a child and then his father as a young man, lived through Nazi occupation and a perilous seminary experience, survived an assassination attempt, and lived with the debilitating effects of Parkinson's disease for many years prior to his death. He never lost faith in the loving hand of the Father and the redemptive power of the cross. Jesus chose to suffer for us and to unite himself with us through this suffering. He loves us and understands when we are in pain, when we grieve, and when we feel hopeless. God, though, is always there. He understands, and he is always there to hold us.

In its ever renewed encounter with man, evangelization is *linked to generational change.* Generations come and go which had distanced themselves from Christ and the Church, which have accepted a secular model of thinking and living or upon which such a model has been imposed. Meanwhile, the Church is always looking toward the future. She constantly *goes out to meet new generations.* And new generations clearly seem to be accepting with enthusiasm what their elders seemed to have rejected. What does this mean? It means that *Christ is forever young.* It means that the Holy Spirit is incessantly at work.[36]

As a priest, St. John Paul II was well known for his connection with young people. He maintained this connection from the time he was a young man himself through the end of his life in his early eighties, which perplexed many onlookers. How could an older man, especially one who began to suffer very publicly from a debilitating illness, be so beloved and relevant among young adults? There was simply something very genuine and passionate about everything that St. John Paul II did. Young people who are searching for meaning and significance in their lives are intuitively drawn to such passion and authenticity. As a result, they found St. John Paul II's affinity for traditional devotions such as the rosary, stations of the cross, and Eucharistic adoration very appealing.

St. John Paul II saw this trend as an indication of Christ and the Church being forever young. He, as Christ's representative on earth, certainly did an outstanding job of making this a reality! The Church and her shepherds must constantly aim to attract young adults. Without them, the Church would lose her vibrancy. To St. John Paul II, Jesus never loses his countercultural message and charm. It is the task of his shepherds to carry on this message via evangelization efforts. Those efforts do not need to be heavy handed or constantly changing and/ or modernized in order to be relevant. Traditional devotions, when shown as passionate examples of a deeply held and meaningful faith, can accomplish this quite nicely. Priests play a role in this evangelization, certainly, but so do we! We can evangelize via our prayers, devotions, and actions, with no words even being necessary. Our everyday faith can be a quiet source of evangelization to others.

In the context of the new evangelization, today's *rediscovery of the authentic values found in popular piety* is very significant. Until fairly recently there was a tendency to look down on popular piety. In our time, however, some of its expressions are experiencing a *true rebirth*—for example, the revival of former pilgrimages and the establishment of new ones.... There exists today the *clear need for a new evangelization. There is the need for a proclamation of the Gospel capable of accompanying man on his pilgrim way, capable of walking alongside the younger generation.*[37]

This selection picks right up where the previous one left off, and, clearly, St. John Paul II wanted to emphasize the role of laypeople in the new evangelization as well as the impact of devotional activities in our everyday lives. Here, he focuses specifically on pilgrimage, and this short segment really touched a chord in my heart. We are all on a pilgrimage, generally speaking, as we navigate our earthly lives toward our heavenly home. This theme of journey speaks to many people, and physically traveling to a holy place is a meaningful spiritual exercise for scores of people throughout their lives. For some, this may be a long trip across an ocean to visit the Holy Land or a Marian apparition site. Others may not be able to travel as far, but it is still very much a pilgrimage to travel only a short distance to a spiritually meaningful site (for example, a local church or shrine, a garden or retreat center dedicated to a saint or person whom you loved). If there is a novena starting soon and your town has a church named for that saint, go there each day for nine days to pray, and bring along a friend who may be curious! This is an excellent, and affordable, form of pilgrimage—and evangelization.

People in all walks of life—those with a strong faith, those struggling with faith, and those with no faith at all—relate to pilgrim journeys. Our invitation to a pilgrimage site, or even simply living out our faith journey in a quietly visible fashion, can be a source of hope and healthy curiosity for others. Our daily emotional journeys, even without ever physically traveling anywhere, are also a form of pilgrimage. Let us endeavor to embrace these opportunities when they come our way!

Totus Tuus. This phrase is not only an expression of piety, or simply an expression of devotion. It is more. During the Second World War, while I was employed as a factory worker, I came to be attracted to Marian devotion. At first, it had seemed to me that I should distance myself a bit from the Marian devotion of my childhood, in order to focus more on Christ. Thanks to Saint Louis of Montfort, I came to understand that true *devotion to the Mother of God is actually Christocentric, indeed, it is very profoundly rooted in the Mystery of the Blessed Trinity,* and the mysteries of the Incarnation and Redemption...In regard to Marian devotion, each of us must understand that such devotion not only addresses a need of the heart, a sentimental inclination, but that it also corresponds to the objective truth about the Mother of God. Mary is the new Eve, placed by God in close relation to Christ, the new Adam, beginning with the Annunciation, through the night of His birth in Bethlehem, through the wedding feast at Cana of Galilee, through the Cross at Calvary, and up to the gift of the Holy Spirit at Pentecost. The Mother of Christ the Redeemer is the Mother of the Church.[38]

St. John Paul II had a deep and abiding devotion to the Mother of God throughout his life, and this devotion is one of the things he is most known for. When he was chosen as pope, he adopted the motto "Totus Tuus," or "totally yours" in reference to Our Lady. To him, Mary was the key to the holy mysteries of our faith: the Incarnation and the Resurrection. Of course, it was Jesus' sacrifice that brought us salvation. But Mary's yes to God's request to be Jesus' mother was integral to all of that taking place.

Mary leads us to Christ. St. John Paul II always emphasized that in his writing, and I experienced that in my own life. When I strayed in my faith, I felt intimidated and afraid to go back to Mass. I did not know how to pray aside from reciting the traditional prayers I had learned in childhood. Asking for Our Lady's intercession in my prayer, on the other hand, seemed incredibly attainable, even soothing. Her motherly embrace made me realize that I did not need to fear turning to my Father. Becoming closer to her brought me closer to her Son.

I have never forgotten that experience, and since that time, I have never been afraid to turn to God in prayer. I credit Mary's motherly intercession for this, and her example has led me in my life from that point forward. Whenever I think of saints who have a strong devotion to Mary, the first to always come to mind is St. John Paul II. Now both of them can intercede for me, and for you.

When, on October 22, 1978, I said the words 'Be not afraid!' in St. Peter's Square, I could not fully know how far they would take me and the entire Church. Their meaning came more from the Holy Spirit, the Consoler promised by the Lord Jesus to His disciples, than from the man who spoke them. Nevertheless, with the passing of the years, I have recalled these words on many occasions...Why should we have no fear? Because man has been redeemed by God. When pronouncing these words in St. Peter's Square, I already knew that my first encyclical and my entire papacy would be tied to the truth of the Redemption. In the Redemption we find the most profound basis for the words 'Be not afraid!': 'For God so loved the world that he gave his only Son' (cf Jn 3:16). This Son is always present in the history of humanity as Redeemer. The Redemption pervades all of human history, even before Christ, and prepares its eschatological future. It is the light that 'shines in the darkness, and the darkness has not overcome it' (cf Jn 1:5). The power of Christ's Cross and Resurrection is greater than any evil which man could or should fear.[39]

One of the reasons I felt such a kinship with St. John Paul II as pope was his exhortation to "Be not afraid!" I am a person who has always been very prone to anxiety, and this situation has only escalated since becoming a mother. Thus, in difficult moments I often think about how challenging a life St. John Paul II led, and yet he tells us to not be afraid. If he could bravely battle his own, very human, fear of death while studying in the underground seminary during the Nazi occupation and while seeing his fellow priests and Jewish countrymen taken to concentration camps, how can I fall prey to fear? I love how St. John Paul II tells us that he did not plan to proclaim this idea, it was a spontaneous nudge of the Holy Spirit! The Holy Spirit knew that so many people needed to hear this message.

Of course, anxiety is a condition that does not go away on command, but I find that meditating on St. John Paul II's admonition does bring me comfort. We have nothing to fear, and the reason for this is the Redemption. We have been redeemed by God, and he will never abandon us. The power of the cross, and of Christ's sacrifice, is stronger than any evil we could face. We may still feel fear, but we can rest easy in the knowledge that God always has our back.

Conclusion

Our study with St. John Paul II was filled with philosophical musings, deep and abiding faith in Catholic devotional practices that lead us to Christ, and passionate exhortations to leave fear behind in our everyday lives. Let us summarize the lessons that we can take away from our time with this powerful and beloved saint.

As a philosopher, St. John Paul II encourages us to ask the deep questions and to have faith that the Lord will answer those questions in prayer, in the Scriptures, and through his shepherds, our priests. God wants us to be curious and to examine our faith and deeply held beliefs, as faith without those things may not withstand the test of time. St. John Paul II assures us that the Lord always understands our doubts and fears, and that he will never abandon us in the anxieties and challenges that life will inevitably bring us.

The Lord also understands our suffering. He sacrificed his Son, who suffered and died a cruel death. When we suffer pain, physical or emotional, the Lord understands and wants to comfort us. We should neither fear turning to him nor doubt that he is there listening to our hurts.

St. John Paul II was also a firm believer in the power of evangelization, but not necessarily through conventional means. He witnessed a resurgence in interest among young people in traditional devotions of the Church: praying the rosary, walking the stations of the cross, and going on pilgrimage, just to mention a few. He encourages us to invite others to accompany us as we do these things, or to simply lead by example.

He fostered a strong devotion to our Blessed Mother throughout his life, and passed that on to his flock as pope, with his stated motto of "Totus Tuus." Mary is a powerful intercessor, and leads us to Christ. She is our mother, and will always provide that motherly touch when we need it.

Finally, St. John Paul II is well known for the words he shared with the world as he accepted the office of the papacy in St. Peter's Square in 1978: "Be not afraid." He encourages us to not live in fear, and to go about our lives in faith and with trust in God's love, mercy, and goodness.

The message of St. John Paul II is one of positivity and hope. I will endeavor to carry his words with me into all my days, and I hope that you will as well!

An Invitation to Ponder

How do I relate to God as father? Do I turn to him when I have an important question about meaning and suffering in my earthly life?

Do I fully trust in God's mercy and goodness, or does fear play a role in my everyday life?

_____

_____

_____

_____

_____

_____

_____

_____

_____

_____

_____

_____

Connecting to Scripture

PRAYER TO THE HOLY SPIRIT BEFORE READING SCRIPTURE

Come, Holy Spirit. Guide me in receiving the message, lovingly personalized just for me, awaiting me here in God's Word. Open my heart to understand and accept what the Scriptures can teach me today. Amen.

🖋 Matthew 4:18–22_____

_____

_____

🖋 Luke 1:39–45 _____

_____

_____

🖋 John 1:1–5 _____

_____

_____

🖋 Romans 5:1–6 _____

_____

_____

🖋 1 Corinthians 9:14–19 _____

_____

_____

⤳ Galatians 4:3–7 _____

_____

_____

Scripture Reflection

Galatians 4:4–5 shows us that we are God's children and heirs: "God sent his Son, born of a woman, born under the law, to ransom those under the law, so that we might receive adoption." God sent his Son, for us, to save us, so that we could become adopted members of the family. Whenever we suffer, we must endeavor to bear this all in mind. To think of the love of our parents for us, or our love for our own children—this is the same love that God has for us too. He gives us free will so that we can choose whether to accept his love, but he always wants us for himself. He can provide the answer or the solace for any question we may have, although we must always take the first step to seek and ask.

Indeed, God loves us so much that he created a plan of salvation for us, and his only Son suffered for us. In Romans 5:1, we learn that "since we have been justified by faith, we have peace with God through our Lord Jesus Christ." Challenges, though, will inevitably appear. We see in verses 3–4 that "affliction produces endurance, and endurance, proven character, and proven character, hope." Jesus embodies this for us. He navigated the difficulties and afflictions that came his way in response to his challenging message, and these afflictions helped to test and solidify his endurance. His endurance then shaped his character and his ability to have hope and faith in his Father. St. John Paul II had hope and faith in his heavenly Father, always, even when losing the most important people in his young life: his parents and brother. The early part of his life involved so much fear, so much oppression, yet his faith was ever steadfast. I think of this often when I am facing something that scares or worries me. St. John Paul II tell us that we should not be afraid because we have the love of God, and we have his Church, always behind us to sustain us.

We should, also, not be afraid to share Jesus' message. St. Paul notes in 1 Corinthians 9:16–18 that he has an obligation to preach the gospel: "and woe to me if I do not preach it!" In so doing, he is rewarded by offering Jesus' message freely to others. Our given role is somewhat different from his, to be sure, but we, too, have the opportunity to share the gospel freely with others. To a reserved person like myself, who places speaking to strangers on the same level as other much more painful things, the words "evangelizing" and "sharing the gospel" sound downright frightening. This experience, however, does not have to be going door-to-door or standing on a street corner wearing a large sign. Living the Christian life is, in and of itself, a form of evangelization! In fact, verse 14 describes, "In the same way, the Lord ordered that those who preach the gospel should live by the gospel." Living out our faith in our daily lives, simply praying a rosary as we walk, tucking a holy card into our book, attending Mass, all of these things are an example to others. This is a way of sharing the faith with other people, and it is just as important as priests preaching an excellent sermon from the pulpit. We want to "win over as many as possible" as described in verse 19, and Christ and his Church need all of us!

Jesus wants to include all of us in his efforts to gather everyone into his Church. In Matthew 4:18–22, we see his short and simple invitation:

"Come after me, and I will make you fishers of men." We may not need to leave our homes and livelihoods the way James, John, Andrew, and Peter did, but Jesus' invitation extends to us too. It is a simple request that requires a yes or no response. Speaking for myself, my answer changes on a daily basis. I say yes a lot more than I say no, but I cannot say that I never say no. We should always be asking ourselves if we are truly following Jesus, and if we are inviting others to follow him as well on our pilgrim journey. Our own pilgrimage can be a source of inspiration to others, and we can pray that we always embrace these opportunities to live out our faith in this way.

God's goodness and strength outperforms any challenge or suffering we could encounter. We do not need to fear what is coming next in our life when we have God's light to look toward. As we see in the beautiful prologue to the Gospel of John, "the light shines in the darkness, and the darkness has not overcome it" (John 1:5). These poetic verses from John 1:1–5 have always been music to my ears, though I have long understood that there is far more happening theologically within the words than I can possibly comprehend. God has always been; he did not need a creator the way that we did. From that beginning, he had a plan for us and for our salvation. He created everything, and nothing in our world would exist without his creating hand. He both created us and redeemed us. To me, this is akin to children resting comfortably, when sick or upset, in the loving arms of their parents. The unpleasantness of the situation still remains, but, somehow, knowing that the other person is there to lovingly hold and protect you makes you feel a million times better.

Of course, our mother, Mary, can aid us in all that we do as we journey on our Christian walk. We see only a few glimpses of Mary in the

Scriptures, but what we do see are quite significant: the annunciation, the crucifixion, the wedding at Cana. We see her in Luke 1:39–45, visiting her cousin Elizabeth, who is due to have a baby much later in her life than anticipated. When we see Mary, she is always very generous. I aim to emulate her generosity of time and spirit, both at home and at my job.

Mary is generous even in her emotions. When others make shocking exclamations to her about her son, such as we see in Luke 1:41–42, with Elizabeth telling Mary that her child leaped in her womb, sensing that Mary was the Mother of the Lord, Mary always reacts with loving and kind words, giving glory to God. She knows when, and how, it is best to speak. She is not impulsive or resentful. She is incredibly worthy of our admiration and our desire to model ourselves after her example.

St. John Paul II's strong devotion to Mary almost certainly ties into the fact that he lost his earthly mother as a young boy. Mary took him under her wing and gave him the motherly guidance he longed for. I am blessed to have a wonderful mother still with me on this earth, but knowing that I also have a mother in heaven is a tremendous source of solace to me. May Mary always intercede for us with her special motherly love.

An Invitation to Share

1. Do you feel that God is present with you when you experience suffering? What types of experiences have members of the group had with God's presence during suffering?

_____

_____

_____

_____

_____

_____

_____

_____

_____

_____

2. In what ways do you evangelize others? Remember, that you do not
   necessarily need to say anything in order to evangelize a fellow seeker!

_____

_____

_____

_____

_____

_____

_____

_____

_____

_____

3. Are there deep questions within our faith that you and other members of the group struggle with?

_____

_____

_____

_____

_____

_____

_____

_____

_____

_____

4. How does St. John Paul II's appeal to "Be not afraid" play a role in your everyday life?

_____

_____

_____

_____

_____

_____

_____

_____

_____

_____

Closing Prayer

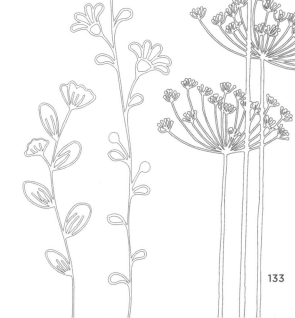

Dear Lord, thank you for the holy and passionate example of St. John Paul II. He was an inspiring and devout gift to the Church during his earthly life, and he continues to be our advocate from the communion of saints. St. John Paul II, please pray for us as we navigate our journey through our earthly lives.

Lord, help us to not be afraid as we discern and live out our vocations, and guide us in always maintaining faith and hope in your love and care. We pray that our lives of faith are an evangelizing example to others, and that we take the time to constantly renew and refresh our faith so that we do not become sedentary or ambivalent. We pray for the passion and devotion to our faith that St. John Paul II showed during his lifetime. We ask this in the precious name of Jesus.

Amen.

7. Abandonment to Divine Providence

Opening Prayer

Dear Lord, we come together to learn more about discerning and accepting your will for our lives. Help us to learn from Fr. Jean-Pierre de Caussade and his wisdom on abandoning ourselves totally to you. Help us, Lord, to strive for a simple faith in your mercy and goodness, and complete trust in your love for us.

Each day, as we go about our daily responsibilities, guide us in emulating Fr. de Caussade, Lord. We long to seek your face in everything that we do, with charity, love, faith, and trust. We want to strive for the complete interior peace that comes from abandoning ourselves to your will for our lives. Let us always see your loving hand in everything that happens to us, and help us to live moment by moment, never becoming consumed with either the past or the future. We ask this in the precious name of Jesus.

Amen.

On My Heart

_____

_____

_____

_____

_____

_____

_____

_____

_____

_____

_____

_____

The Blessing of Fr. Jean-Pierre de Caussade

Fr. Jean-Pierre de Caussade lived in France during the sixteenth and seventeenth centuries and is someone I was unfamiliar with until picking up *Abandonment to Divine Providence.* He was a devout young man who became a Jesuit priest and, ultimately, the spiritual director for a convent of Visitation nuns in Nancy, France. The nuns collected his letters and notes from the conferences he provided for them, and those letters and notes are the source of the text for *Abandonment to Divine Providence.* These compiled works were published under this title over one hundred years following Fr. de Caussade's death.

Although he was a Jesuit, Fr. de Caussade was heavily influenced by Carmelite spirituality, having taken a shine to the works of St. John of the Cross. Fr. de Caussade's emphasis on simplicity in spirituality and his focus on abandoning oneself in faith and trust in the Lord led to a hypothesis that St. Thérèse of Lisieux may have been influenced by him. She was alive in the nineteenth century shortly after *Abandonment to Divine Providence* made its debut, and her "little way" and emphasis on smallness certainly bear a resemblance to Fr. de Caussade's teachings.

Fr. de Caussade is known for his deep faith in abandonment to God's will. He was a firm believer in living life from moment to moment, never allowing oneself to become consumed with either the past or the future. We must live out what God is asking us to do at this moment without worrying about anything else. Given my propensity to lack trust in God and give in to anxiety, I am very eager to learn from Fr. de Caussade's wisdom as a spiritual director!

**Reflection on Selections
from** *Abandonment to Divine Providence*

> If a faithful soul accepts God's will and purpose in all simplicity, he will reach perfection without ever realizing it, just as a sick man who swallows his medicine obediently will be cured, although he neither knows nor cares about medicine. We need know nothing about the chemistry of combustion to enjoy the warmth of a fire. Holiness is produced in us by the will of God and our acceptance of it. It is not produced by intellectual speculation about it. If we are thirsty we must have a drink and not worry about books which explain what thirst is. If we waste time seeking an explanation about thirst, all that will happen is that we shall get thirstier. It is the same when we thirst after

holiness. The desire to know more about it will only drive it further away. We must put all speculation aside and, with childlike willingness, accept all that God presents to us. What God arranges for us to experience at each moment is the best and holiest thing that could happen to us.[40]

Fr. de Caussade's ministry was devoted to a complete abandonment of self to God's will for our lives, and to a constant striving to be in closer union with him. Here, he is telling us that it is in our best interest to not only accept God's will, but to accept it without question. He even uses the word "childlike," a type of faith we covered quite extensively with St. Thérèse, and it very aptly applies here as well. A childlike obedience and willingness to accept what God is asking of us, without demanding an explanation or reason for why things turn out the way that they do. As I am certain we all know, this is no easy task.

When I first read Fr. de Caussade's words that "the desire to know more about it will only drive it further away," I wondered to myself briefly whether he was saying that an inquisitive and curious nature about our faith was a bad thing. That struck me as worrisome because I am in fact very inquisitive and curious! In matters of faith, I think that part of solidifying our faith and making that transition from a childhood faith into an adult one is studying and learning about it on one's own. In fact, though, I think that what Fr. de Caussade is telling us is that while we can and should be intellectually curious about our faith, we should not *need* to be curious in order to accept God's will. Our acceptance of his plan for us should not come with caveats or prerequisites. Acceptance is abandonment, complete and total.

This type of acceptance involves a great trust, it is true. Trust that what God is asking of us is the "best and holiest thing that could happen to us." I know this in my mind, but I do not always hold it in my heart. This is a very human characteristic and why I, along with many others, struggle with faith and trust. We can all aspire to something greater, though, and all that God asks of us is that we keep trying.

All creatures live in the hand of God. By our senses we can see only the action of the creature, but faith sees the creator acting in all things. Faith sees that Jesus Christ lives in everything and works through all history to the end of time, that every fraction of a second, every atom of matter, contains a fragment of his hidden life and his secret activity. The actions of created beings are veils which hide the profound mysteries of the workings of God. After the Resurrection, Jesus Christ took the disciples unawares by his appearances, showing himself to them as if disguised and then appearing when he had revealed himself. And it is this same Jesus, ever living and ever active, who still surprises us if our faith is not strong and clear-sighted enough. There is never a moment when God does not come forward in the guise of some suffering or some duty, and all that takes place within us, around us and through us both includes and hides his activity. Yet, because it is invisible, we are always taken by surprise and do not recognize his operation until it has passed by us. If we could lift the veil and if we watched with vigilant attention, God would endlessly reveal himself to us and we should see and rejoice in his active presence in all that befalls us.[41]

"Sometimes you need to see the forest, rather than just the trees." Someone has said this to you at some point, yes? If you are me, your mother may have said this to you over the years more times than there are stars in the sky. Fr. de Caussade is alluding to the same con-

cept here. Things happen to us as we move about our day, and sometimes these things are upsetting or challenging. If we were to trust
deeply enough, we would know that even in these difficult moments,
God is still there. Not only that but also that he loves us and wants to
bring us closer to himself.

I often agonize over the minutiae of my day, struggling with faith and
trust, and in making decisions to resolve various situations. If I were to
step back more often, I would see that these things are not mere annoyances or meaningless encounters brought about just to frustrate
me. God is there, in every single instance. I may not see him, but he
is always there. I need to trust in that truth and in the fact that even
amid suffering, he is there to comfort us, and to bring us to himself
through these circumstances.

If we wish to enjoy an abundance of blessings we have only
one thing to do: purify our hearts by emptying them of all desire for created things and surrender ourselves wholly to God.
By doing this we shall get all we want...Through the ardor of
our faith we see God as he is. We see him in everything and at
every moment working within and around us. And in all things
we are both his subject and his instrument. He guides us everywhere and leads us to everything. Very often we do not think
about it, but he thinks for us. It is enough that we have desired
what is happening to us and must happen to us by his will. He
understands our readiness. We are bewildered and seek to find
this desire within ourselves, but we cannot. He, though, sees it
very clearly...If we are going eastward, he makes us turn to the
west. If we are about to run onto the rocks, he takes the helm

and brings us into port. We have neither map nor compass, know nothing of winds or tides, yet we always make a prosperous voyage. If pirates try to board us, an unexpected gust of wind sweeps us beyond their reach.[42]

God keeps a loving hand on us as we move through life, granting us our free will, but also guiding us. Though we have free will, we can surrender ourselves to God and try to live wholly within his plan for us. We can always either choose God or choose to go another way, and Fr. de Caussade reminds us that joy awaits us in choosing God and surrendering ourselves to his embrace.

I love Fr. de Caussade's imagery of God guiding us through the journey of life: "If we are about to run onto the rocks, he takes the helm and brings us into port." As he mentioned in the previous selection, we do not see the larger picture the way that God does (with him having the map and compass and with us wandering in the forest a bit more aimlessly), but we do not need to worry. Ultimately, God is there to save us. We may sometimes make poor choices—not the ones God wishes that we would make—but in the end, we can achieve salvation because of him and be with him forever.

For me, this is a comforting way of thinking. We are not promised an easy time of things here on earth, but God is always there for us in the midst of it all. We just have to be willing to recognize that he is there, despite not being able to physically see him. We have to be willing to accede our decisions, in prayer, to what we believe God would have us do. It is our willingness that is at issue, our surrender of control to him. We are still steering the ship, but God is the breeze, guiding us as we sail.

Never mind weariness, illness, lack of feeling, irritability, exhaustion, the snares of the devil and of men, with all that they create of distrust, jealousy, prejudice and evil imaginings. Let us soar like an eagle above these clouds, with our eyes fixed on the sun and its rays, which are our duties. We cannot help being aware of all these evils, of course, and we cannot be indifferent to them, but let us never forget that ours is not a life governed by our feelings. We must live in those upper reaches of the spiritual life where God and his will are active in a process which is eternal and unchanging...Here on earth we suffer—to use the language of allegory—the attacks of monsters, owls and savage beasts. But terrible though these attacks are, behind them God is acting and giving us something of the divine which will give us the brilliance of the sun, for here below both body and soul are refined and fashioned like gold and iron, linen and gems. Like these things, they will not attain their full beauty until they have been trimmed and shaped and changed from their original form. All they have endured in this life at the hand of God—and he is love itself—is meant only to prepare them for eternal bliss.[43]

"Ours is not a life governed by our feelings." For a sensitive, emotional person like myself, these words really hit home! Very often, on a daily basis even, I am governed by my feelings. Hurt feelings and feelings of insecurity, of joy and melancholy, of anxiety and worry—all of these make up a portion of my days. I had to chuckle at Fr. de Caussade's own list: "weariness, illness, lack of feeling, irritability, exhaustion, the snares of the devil and of men" In fact, I have small children so I should add a few of these to my list as well!

As we move through our lives, we are going to suffer. We will suffer because of things on the lists I mentioned above, and we will suffer because of death and other tragedies. As we endure all of these things, they will strengthen us. They will bring us closer to the Lord if we allow them to. It is very difficult to do, but if are willing to put our sights on God, rather than allowing our feelings to rule our actions, we can transcend the suffering. We are human, and, of course, we are going to experience and express emotion. We can, however, channel that emotion to a longing for God that will bring us closer to our ultimate home in heaven.

To live by faith is to live joyfully, to live with assurance, untroubled by doubts and with complete confidence in all we have to do and suffer at each moment by the will of God. We must realize that it is in order to stimulate and sustain this faith that God allows the soul to be buffeted and swept away by the raging torrent of so much distress, so many troubles, so much embarrassment and weakness, and so many setbacks. For it is essential to have faith to find God behind all this. The divine life is neither seen nor felt, but there is never a moment when it is not acting in an unknown but very sure manner. It is hidden under such things as death of the body, damnation of the soul, and the general disorder of all earthly affairs. Faith is nourished and strengthened by these happenings.[44]

It is such a simple thing at this point in our journey together through Scripture and through the spiritual classics, but yet so complex at the same time: faith. If you are reading this Scripture study, you very likely have faith in God. That is an outstanding starting point, but, as we know, maintaining faith throughout long stretches of time, as one moves through different seasons of life, is not a guaranteed thing.

Fr. de Caussade reminds us, yet again, that faith is not seen or felt, but, nevertheless, it is always there. We can and should act as if it is always there, even when we feel bereft emotionally. Seeing death, suffering, and destruction can certainly instill a feeling of hopelessness in a person. Despite this, our faith is always there. Once we have said yes to God, that faith never leaves us. It may be buried very deep down in our consciousness, but it is there, lying in wait for us to reach for it again. God is always using our circumstances to strengthen us and draw us closer to him. Even when our efforts at faith feel a bit like a clawing desperation, God does not mind this. Our goal is to live by our faith and to try to see the joy in everything. Where there is God, there is joy.

For it is impossible for God to guide a soul without giving it the certainty that it is on the right path, a conviction which is greater the less it is perceived, and one which conquers all fear and the reasoning of the mind. It is in vain that the intellect protests and struggles to find a better way. The bride senses the presence of the bridegroom without feeling him, for when she tries to touch him he disappears. 'His right arm embraces her' (Song of Songs 2:6) and she prefers to abandon herself to his guidance, even though it seems without rhyme or reason, rather than try to reassure herself by struggling along the beaten paths of virtue. So come, my soul, come and let us go to God by self-abandonment. Let us acknowledge that we are incapable of becoming holy by our own efforts, and put our trust in God, who would not have taken away our ability to walk unless he was to carry us in his arms.[45]

This verse calls to mind the image that we are all likely familiar with: the scene of footprints in the sand, with the single set of prints at one point being an indication of Jesus carrying us through particularly difficult periods of time. When we have God with us, we are never abandoned, and we are never alone. So often, we struggle with our faith because we want full control over what happens to us. Even for those with a completely secular mindset, having control over everything that happens is, of course, an impossibility. It is better for us to accept that we have very limited control over what happens in our lives, and to acknowledge that God is there to guide us. We should rest comfortably with that knowledge.

I have to give Fr. de Caussade credit for saying what we are all thinking: "Let us acknowledge that we are incapable of becoming holy by our own efforts." There is a limit to what we are capable of via our own intentions. With God, however, all things are possible. When we do not have the ability to walk, God will carry us in his arms. When we call this to mind, we have nothing to fear.

Conclusion

My time with Fr. de Caussade's work was a complete surprise to me. Based on the title of this book, I was expecting a heavy read and to have difficulty applying his words to my own spiritual experience. A gal with a short attention span and a propensity to oversleep in the mornings rather than rise early for morning prayer is not exactly known for her above average ability to abandon herself to divine providence. I was in for quite a shock. Fr. de Caussade's words spoke to my soul, and all of these weeks later, I am still thinking about them. Let us take a quick look back on his advice to us.

Fr. de Caussade's mission was to preach abandonment of ourselves to God's will for our lives. To this end, he advised that a childlike obedience to God and acceptance of God's plan for us is infinitely better than anything we could ever imagine for ourselves. Such a grand achievement requires absolute trust in God's authority, goodness, and love for us. So often, we see only the small challenges and roadblocks of each day and want a quick resolution to them. God, though, sees the big picture and grand plan for us, which likely requires a much more long-term resolution. Only our trust can make this a reality for us. The more we struggle against what God has in store for us, the more frustration and angst we will cause ourselves.

Throughout our lives, God is there beside us, even though we do not always see or feel him at any given moment. God will lovingly guide us through the sea of life if we hold out our hand to him in love and trust. Fr. de Caussade's words about God guiding our ship into port calls to my mind an image of Our Lady, Star of the Sea. Our Lady, Star of the Sea is an ancient title for Mary in which she guides and protects seafarers on their stormy and dangerous journeys. Our Lady is our intercessor and will lead us to Christ. And Christ will guide us home.

Fr. de Caussade also advises that we try not to allow ourselves to be ruled by emotion but, instead, by love and desire for God. We are emotional creatures, but it is important to recognize that our emotions often get us into further difficulty, rather than out of it. If we channel that emotion into love for our Creator, we can then allow him to transform our lives.

In the end, we must have faith. It is such a simple concept that may come naturally to all of us participating in this Scripture study, but yet it is complex in application. Each and every day, we must have faith that God loves us and will take care of us. We are limited in what we can accomplish on our own, and we cannot become holy on our own! With God, though, all things are possible.

An Invitation to Ponder

What is the most comforting image of God that I can picture? How can I incorporate that image into my daily time of meditation? How well do I abandon myself to God's will? In what way(s) do I struggle on a daily basis with having faith and trust in what God is asking me to do?

_____

_____

_____

_____

_____

_____

_____

_____

_____

_____

_____

_____

_____

_____

_____

_____

Connecting to Scripture

PRAYER TO THE HOLY SPIRIT BEFORE READING SCRIPTURE

Come, Holy Spirit. Guide me in receiving the message, lovingly personalized just for me, awaiting me here in God's Word. Open my heart to understand and accept what the Scriptures can teach me today. Amen.

❧ Psalm 4 _____

_____

_____

❧ Proverbs 8:29-30 _____

_____

_____

❧ Ecclesiastes 12:13-14 _____

_____

_____

❧ Matthew 19:24-26 _____

_____

_____

✐ John 21:1-7 _____

_____

_____

✐ Romans 8:28-30 _____

_____

_____

Scripture Reflection

Fr. de Caussade's teaching focuses heavily on total abandonment to God's will. A childlike faith is simple, but powerful. Ecclesiastes provides us with a beautiful simplicity in this regard: we should "fear God and keep his commandments." God asks us to have no other gods before him, to obey the important behavioral rules he sets before us, and to keep the Sabbath day holy. To have a deep and abiding faith in God and his plans for us, we have to trust him. We may struggle with this, but it all comes down to trust. It is a simple thing, but a multifaceted one. It is simple in our minds, but complex in our hearts. Reading God's Word helps me to focus on the straightforwardness of what he lays out for us. I do not need to make things so difficult for myself by worrying, questioning God, and giving in to anxiety and despair. Trust actually eases our minds rather than heightening our fears. It may take some time to reach that level, but it is there for us should we choose to aspire to it.

Even the disciples struggled with faith and trust. In John 21:1–7, I love how it takes the disciples a little time to realize that it is Jesus speaking to them and not someone whom they do not recognize. When the miraculous load of fish appear, after an unsuccessful day on the water, only then does one person catch on. "It is the Lord." He passes the word on quietly so that this friends will become attuned to what is happening as well. They are in this confusing situation together, and he wants to help his friends out.

How frequently does this happen to us? It happens to me countless times, and sometimes I still fail to recognize the Lord at work in the events of my day. Sometimes, though, I will be huffing about, frustrated that the monitor on the instructor workstation in my classroom is mysteriously failing to come on yet again, and I'll be sweating it out because class is about to begin. But then I will take a moment to realize that a grand conspiracy is not afoot. It is a simple issue, if a frustrating one, and I should calmly call my colleagues over to troubleshoot with me. While I wait for them, a student will approach me with a problem that they were afraid to ask about before. The extra time before class began, which was a result of the technical delay, provided enough time for that student to work up the courage to come and ask me. In those moments, I realize that God is hard at work in every situation. He can bring good out of anything, and he is there, if only we will let him in.

Trust has been a strong theme throughout our time with Fr. de Caussade, and Psalm 4:2 is the perfect prayer for us when we need to call upon that trust to get us through our day: "Answer me when I call, my saving God. When troubles hem me in, set me free; take pity on me, hear my prayer." When we call upon the Lord, we want him to hear and answer us. We want to feel the peace of the Lord fill our hearts as we drift off to sleep at night, secure in his love and care. We are like children in this way, wanting to sleep in the comforting and safe embrace of our parent.

The Psalms often provide the ideal inspiration for our prayer lives when we need an uplifting session with the Lord. Let the entirety of Psalm 4 guide us as we strive to increase our prayer and grow in trust in the Lord. Trust is not something we can attain without regularly stumbling and failing. We simply need to be willing to try again whenever we fail.

Our efforts will not go unnoticed. Romans 8:28 instructs us that "all things work for good for those who love God." It may not feel that way sometimes, but the Scriptures tell us this. For those of us who love the Lord, God has called us. It feels special to be called, does it not? God calls us, he has justified us, and he has glorified us. That is certainly a weighty undertaking for us to contemplate. It does, however, show God's incredible love for us. Faith and love, these two things go together perfectly, and the Scriptures have wedded them together for us. Christ shows us the ideal example. He lived a life filled with difficulty and suffering for us, and then he died for us, all while clinging to the love and promises of his Father. We can have this, too, if we hang on to our faith and recall God's love for us through every moment.

Our faith is crucial for our salvation, but we cannot attain salvation by our own merits. The Scriptures show Jesus explaining this to his disciples via the example of a very rich man in Matthew 19:24. It will be very difficult for this man to enter the kingdom of heaven because it is very easy for him to become so concerned about his possessions that he neglects God and his fellow man. The disciples are very upset by this story, and they are asking Jesus who, given how apparently difficult it is, can be saved.

Jesus wastes no time in letting them know that if it were all up to us, no one would be saved. Regardless of our intentions, we often manage to make a mess of things, do we not? "For human beings this is impossible, but for God all things are possible," he tells us in Matthew

19:26. He has saved us, he can guide us, and he loves us. We just need to be willing to follow him.

Our willingness to obey our Father harkens back to our original analysis of Fr. de Caussade's discussion of childlike faith. Proverbs 8:29-30 perfectly exemplifies our loving parent–child relationship to the Father in heaven. We do delight God by our willingness to be there beside him, playing at his feet: "I was his delight day by day, playing before him all the while." This is such an enchanting view of our trust in God as our ultimate father figure and of the parental role God plays in our lives. This is yet another indication that God loves us and is always there for us. It can be difficult to remember this from day to day, but if we can find a prayer, or even repeat this Scripture verse, to remind ourselves of this fact, it will add meaning to our daily routines without fail.

An Invitation to Share

1. Among the group members, what are some examples of times when God had a larger, grander plan in mind, but it took a long while for that resolution to become clear? How can we learn about trust from these examples?

_____

_____

_____

_____

_____

_____

_____

_____

_____

_____

_____

_____

2. What words come to mind when you hear the phrase, "abandonment to God's will"? What are ways that we can incorporate these words into our everyday lives?

_____

_____

_____

_____

_____

_____

_____

_____

_____

_____

_____

_____

_____

3. In what ways are we easily ruled by our emotions? What are strategies that we can use to overcome this?

_____

_____

_____

_____

_____

_____

_____

_____

_____

4. What does a life of faith look like for women living in the twenty-first century? How can we work to strengthen our faith on a daily basis?

_____

_____

_____

_____

_____

_____

_____

_____

_____

Closing Prayer

Dear Lord, thank you for the beautiful wisdom of Fr. de Caussade that transcends the centuries to reach us here today. His words are powerful Lord—at the same time simple, as well as incredibly complex. You alone, Lord, can guide us through the sea of life, and we long to trust you completely. Help us to build that trust with you, Lord. Guide us in a Christian life of faith, hope, and love as we make our way through these earthly challenges, all the while wanting to be with you in eternity when our time here is complete.

We know, Lord, that we can only accomplish things through you, and that nothing is impossible for you. We pray for the wisdom to discern the larger plan that you have in mind for us, and to not become frustrated and emotional with our smaller, earthly perspective. Lord, increase our faith. Our Lady, Star of the Sea, pray for us. We ask this in the precious name of Jesus.

Amen.

Endnotes

1 Thomas á Kempis, *The Imitation of Christ*, trans. Joseph N. Tylenda, S.J., (New York: Vintage, 1998), Book I, chapter 11, p. 13.

2 á Kempis, *Imitation*, Book II, chapter 10, p. 61.

3 á Kempis, *Imitation*, Book II, chapter 10, p. 61.

4 á Kempis, *Imitation*, Book III, chapter 11, p. 91.

5 á Kempis, *Imitation*, Book III, chapter 11, pp. 91–92.

6 á Kempis, *Imitation*, Book IV, chapter 10, pp. 198–99.

7 For more information on the other titles available in the *Stay Connected* series, visit www.gracewatch.media.

8 á Kempis, *Imitation*, Book III, chapter 11, p. 91.

9 á Kempis, *Imitation*, Book IV, chapter 10, p. 198.

10 Thérèse of Lisieux, *The Autobiography of Saint Thérèse of Lisieux: The Story of a Soul*, trans. John Beevers (New York: Doubleday, 2001), 1—2.

11 Thérèse of Lisieux, *Story of a Soul*, pp. 2–3.

12 Thérèse of Lisieux, *Story of a Soul*, p. 113.

13 Thérèse of Lisieux, *Story of a Soul*, p, 113.

14 Thérèse of Lisieux, *Story of a Soul*, pp. 139–40.

15 Thérèse of Lisieux, *Story of a Soul*, p. 121.

16 Teresa of Avila, *The Way of Perfection*, trans. E. Allison Peers, (New York: Image Books, 2004), chapter X, p. 66.

17 Teresa of Avila, *Perfection*, chapter X, pp. 66–67.

18 Teresa of Avila, *Perfection*, chapter XXI, p. 135.

19 Teresa of Avila, *Perfection*, chapter XXVI, pp. 161–62.

20 Teresa of Avila, *Perfection*, chapter XXVII, pp. 168–69.

21 Teresa of Avila, *Perfection*, chapter XXXVII, p. 246.

22 St. Francis de Sales, *Introduction to the Devout Life*, ed. and abridged Msgr. Charles Dollen, (New York: Alba Books, 1992), Part One, chapter 5, pp. 11–12.

23 de Sales, *Devout Life*, Part One, chapter 19, p. 34.

24 de Sales, *Devout Life*, Part Two, chapter 8, p. 51.

25 de Sales, *Devout Life*, Part Three, chapter 10, p. 94.

26 de Sales, *Devout Life*, Part Three, chapter 35, pp. 129–30.

27 de Sales, *Devout Life*, Part Four, chapter 12, p. 155.

28 Edith Stein, *Essays on Woman*, trans. Freda Mary Oben, (Washington: ICS Publications, 1996), chapter I, p. 49.

29 Stein, *Woman*, chapter II, p. 84.

30 Stein, *Woman*, chapter III, p. 125.

31 Stein, *Woman*, chapter IV, pp. 144–45.

32 Stein, *Woman*, chapter IV, p. 145.

33 Stein, *Woman*, chapter VI, p. 241.

34 John Paul II, *Crossing the Threshold of Hope*, ed. Vittorio Messori, (New York: Knopf, 1995), p. 30.

35 John Paul II, *Threshold of Hope*, p. 66.

36 John Paul II, *Threshold of Hope*, p. 113.

37 John Paul II, *Threshold of Hope*, pp. 116–17.

38 John Paul II, *Threshold of Hope*, pp. 212–13.

39 John Paul II, *Threshold of Hope*, pp. 218–19.

40 Jean-Pierre de Caussade, *Abandonment to Divine Providence*, trans. John Beevers, (New York: Doubleday, 1975), chapter I, pp. 26–27.

41 de Caussade, *Abandonment*, chapter II, p. 36.

42 de Caussade, *Abandonment*, chapter III, pp. 68–69.

43 de Caussade, *Abandonment*, chapter IV, pp. 73–74.

44 de Caussade, *Abandonment*, chapter V, pp. 95–96.

45 de Caussade, *Abandonment*, chapter VI, p. 100.